From Plotzk to Boston

MASTERWORKS OF MODERN JEWISH WRITING SERIES
EDITED BY JONATHAN D. SARNA

Academic Director of the Center for the Study of American Jewish Experience
Hebrew Union College—Jewish Institute of Religion

From Plotzk to Boston

BY MARY ANTIN

With a new introduction by
Pamela S. Nadell
American University

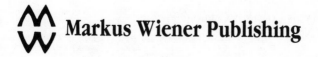 **Markus Wiener Publishing**

First Markus Wiener Publishing edition 1986

For information write to:
Markus Wiener Publishing, Inc.
2901 Broadway, New York, N.Y. 10025

Cover design by Cheryl Mirkin

ISBN 0-910129-45-2

Library of Congress Catalog
Card No. 85-040728

INTRODUCTION

by *Pamela S. Nadell*

In the town of Polotzk,[1] part of a world that is no more, in the Russian Pale of Settlement on June 13, 1881, a little girl named Maryashe was born to Israel Pinchus and Esther Weltman (Hannah Hayye) Antin.[2] Her father was the only son of the glazier and peddler Joseph of Yuchovitch and his wife Rachel Kimanyer, the daughter of the sainted Hasid Israel Kimanyer. Rachel, although greatly impoverished, had scrimped and saved, determined to see her one and only son become a great scholar. When the time came to find a bride for him, she proposed Hannah Hayye, the only daughter of the prosperous businessman Raphael the Russian and his wife, Deborah. At the age of fifteen Hannah was already adept at serving customers in the family's dry goods store. Moreover, she was bright, capable, well educated, and of an age when Jewish girls in Polotzk became brides.

The marriage fulfilled both families' expectations. In Israel, Raphael acquired a scholar for a son-in-law. And in marrying Hannah Hayye, Israel Pinchus gained a father-in-law, who promised him several years of room and board free from the burden of supporting a wife and children. This dowry gift would enable Israel to complete his studies to become the scholar he had always been told he would be. Such were the marriage arrangements among traditional Jews in the world of the *shtetl*.

A year after the wedding two changes came to pass. The first was to be expected. Hannah Hayye gave birth to the first of her six children, her daughter Fetchke (Fanny in *From Plotzk to Boston*). The second transformation—Israel's growing disenchantment with the life of the scholar—had not been anticipated. When his waywardness became evident, his father-in-law withdrew his support, forcing him to make his own way in the world. Shouldering the responsibility for his growing family—a second child, Maryashe (Mary Antin) had recently been born—Israel Pinchus embarked on several enterprises, only to fail at each one in turn.

When Mary was four, the Antins' financial situation suddenly improved. Grandfather Raphael died, leaving the family business to his daughter Hannah. Profiting from her youthful experience in the store and aided by her husband, Hannah made the business flourish. Mary's early childhood memories confirm the well-being that came from this new-found prosperity. Busy all day at the store, the Antins employed servants to care for their house and growing family—now including Mary's only brother, Joseph, and the baby Deborah (Dora).[3] Prosperity also meant that Joseph could go to school and that tutors could be hired to teach Fetchke and Mary such subjects as Hebrew, Russian, German, and arithmetic.

But these happy days of childhood proved fleeting. Illness struck first Israel, then several of his children, and finally Hannah, who remained bedridden for more than two long years. Medical bills undermined the family fortune; bad management by those left in charge of the business caused its collapse. The Antins were ruined.

Their plight, however pathetic, was not unique. Over the course of the nineteenth century life had become increasingly intolerable for Russian Jewry. Economic problems of one sort or another gradually impoverished much of the community.

Then came the violent pogroms. They did not reach as far as Polotzk while the Antins lived there. Still, animosity between Jews and Russians ran high, forcing the Antins periodically to cower behind locked doors, trembling from fear of the local peasants. Finally, on top of this, the Russian authorities enacted tougher and more restrictive economic and residential legislation, making it still more difficult for the Jews to eke out a living. In 1891, just before Passover, authorities expelled the most privileged Jews in the Empire from Moscow, forcing them back into the Pale of Settlement. That Passover some Jews of Polotzk replaced the words "Next year—in America" for the traditional prayer "Next year in Jerusalem." Mary Antin's father, ruined and fearful, recognized as did hundreds of thousands of Russian Jews, that there was no hope left for him in the Empire. So he kissed his wife and children goodbye and set off for America, there to better his fortune. It was understood that he would send passage tickets for the rest of the family as soon as he could afford them.

For three years Hannah bore alone the burden for the care of her children. Averting her eyes when she passed by neighbors who had known her in her days of prosperity, she peddled tea and other wares to keep bread on the table and creditors at bay. Fetchke and Mary no longer studied, instead they were apprenticed out to work. Mary, her sister's junior by two years, was weak and often sickly and was soon sent home, as she was of little use in the milliner's workroom. Fetchke, however, proved skillful at dressmaking. That skill would, in a few short years, propel her into the factories of Boston, even as her younger sister followed a different path.

America disappointed Israel Antin: it was not paved with

gold. But after three years he was able to borrow enough money to send ships' tickets to Polotzk for his wife and children. The five remaining Antins left Polotzk for Boston in the early spring of 1894, when Mary was thirteen years old, and landed in America some six weeks later.

The change in family fortune did not bring about a corresponding change in family finances. Once again Israel opened and closed several businesses. A refreshment stand at Revere Beach took the Antins to the seaside for their first summer in America, but trouble about a license abruptly ended that venture. Next Mary's father opened a grocery store on the outskirts of Boston in Chelsea, but selling on credit to the impoverished Jews, Blacks, and Irish who frequented the store soon brought on ruin. Finally, the Antins were forced to settle in the slums of Boston's South End, moving from one tenement to another, always in debt to the grocer and the landlady. Like other immigrant families they found that they could only make ends meet by putting all capable hands to work. What meager living the Antins made came from the combined earnings of Israel's labor, Fanny's dressmaking, and Joseph's newspaper sales.

There was, however, one bright spot in this otherwise gloomy tale of immigrant hardship. For although America did not deliver on its promise of prosperity to the Antins, it did deliver on its promise of equal opportunity. Education kept the American dream alive for the next generation. In Polotzk, Israel's great plans for his children's education had been quashed by poverty and by the Russian school authorities, who refused to educate an impoverished Jewish child at public expense. But America was different. Here public education was free for the taking. Here the Antin children could be educated as Americans. Fanny was of working age and her income could not be spared, so she remained behind in the shops. Mary, Joseph, and Dora, however, marched proudly off to school, led by their father.

Years later Mary Antin captured the moment when they crossed that sacred threshold.

> So it was with a heart full of longing and hope that my father led us to school on that first day. At last the four of us stood around the teacher's desk; and my father, in his impossible English, gave us over in her charge, with some broken word of his hopes for us that his swelling heart could no longer contain.... This foreigner who brought his children to school as if it were an act of consecration, who regarded the teacher of the primer class with reverence, who spoke of visions, like a man inspired, in a common schoolroom, was not like other aliens ... I think Miss Nixon guessed what my father's best English could not convey. I think she divined that by the simple act of delivering our school certificates to her he took possession of America.[4]

These words conveyed not only Israel's reverence for the American public school, but most assuredly that of Mary Antin—for it was the public school that opened up America to her. It transformed the foreign-born immigrant child Maryashe into Mary Antin, author, confidante of an American president, and interpreter of the immigrant experience to her fellow countrymen.

Like other immigrant children in the days when grade levels were determined by competence in English rather than age, thirteen-year-old Antin squeezed herself into a desk meant for the kindergarten and prepared to learn what America was all about. Her intelligence, rapid progress in learning English, and literary gifts quickly became apparent, especially to her third grade teacher, Mary Dillingham. Impressed with her pupil's progress and impatient to demonstrate to a wider audience how much an eager immigrant child could accomplish in but four months, Dillingham sent Antin's composition, "Snow," to *Primary Education*. Seeing her name in print for the first time, Antin felt that "[n]othing so wonderful had ever happened to me before. My whole consciousness was suddenly transformed. I suppose that was the moment when I became a writer."

Mary Antin continued her rapid progress. By the middle of her second year in Boston, she was promoted to the sixth grade. There, in studying for the first time the heroes of the American Revolution, she began to plumb the depths of American patriotism. She found herself worshipping Washington and the Revolutionary patriots who had striven at great sacrifice to defy their oppressors in defense of *"my country."* She embraced willingly the rights and privileges of citizenship, thrilling to know that it also demanded responsibilities. At the same time, she found that her Jewish heritage paled before the American past that now belonged to her. The Bible told of an independent, glorious Jewish kingdom, but that was ancient history. Centuries of hatred, persecution, and exile had tarnished black that once radiant memory. Although Mary sang with her father and sister of the rebuilding of Zion, she did not expect to see it in her lifetime, nor could she envision abandoning her adopted homeland for a restored Judea. For Antin, and for the immigrant thousands whose voice she became, America had become Zion.

Americanization rapidly made headway in the Antin household as well. One Sabbath in Polotzk, Mary had watched her father surreptitiously turn out the lamp, violating the commandment to refrain from extinguishing fire on the holy day of rest. In Boston, therefore, she was not surprised to find her father dispense with the outward forms of Jewish observance that impeded his push to Americanize his greenhorn family. In fact, the Antins' Americanization really began even before they left Polotzk. Along with the family's ships' tickets, Israel had sent a command to Hannah to discard on the far side of the ocean her matronly *sheitl*, the wig that modestly covered a married Jewish woman's hair. Subsequent changes in the home and the lessons learned in school left Mary with a watered-down view of things Jewish. She concluded that she "could honor God by loving her neighbor, which is perhaps not far from being the whole of Judaism."

Guided by her teachers, Mary Antin vaulted through grammar school in four years. At the same time she began to fulfill the ambition that had been born when she first saw her name in print. Publication of her poems in such newspapers as the *Boston Herald* and the *Transcript* made her a local celebrity. The young writer was befriended by the prominent Bostonian Edward Everett Hale and by Hattie L. Hecht, a local Jewish communal leader. At her grammar school graduation in 1898, her remarkable career was held up "as an illustration of what the American system of free education and the European immigrant could make of each other." To those who championed the nation's capacity to assimilate the immigrant and the immigrant's capacity to enrich America, Mary Antin became a symbol.

Encouraged by her teachers and her friends to prepare for college and by her father who shared their hopes despite the family's poverty, Antin enrolled in the Girls' Latin School in Boston. Knowing of the family's desperate plight and of its need to put all hands to work to make ends meet, Hattie L. Hecht persuaded Philip Cowen, the editor of the *American Hebrew*, to arrange for the publication of Antin's first book, entitled, owing to a misprint, *From Plotzk to Boston*.[5] He underwrote the volume which appeared in 1899, when Mary was eighteen.

Before she began writing in English, Mary Antin had been an inveterate letter writer in her native Yiddish, honing her literary skills in letters to her father during their long separation. When the Antins left Polotzk in 1894, one of Mary's uncles, knowing of her gift for letters, made her promise to write him an account of their journey to Boston. In the summer of 1894 at the age of thirteen she wrote the letters that became *From Plotzk to Boston*, later translating the account into English.[6] The book quickly sold out its first printing and was favorably reviewed. Cowen later speculated that Mrs. Hecht artificially stimulated sales with her own multiple purchases. The income from the book enabled Antin to continue at the Girls' Latin School and to dream of the not-too-distant day when she might attend college, perhaps even Radcliffe.

School, writing, household chores, and visits with her recently married sister Fanny did not occupy all of Antin's time. For recreation and to enhance her education, she joined a natural history club at the Hale House, a South End settlement home. There Antin found her eyes opened to "the wonder and thrill of the revelations of science, till all my thoughts became colored with the tints of infinite truths." Natural studies revealed an orderly and complex universe that was far wider than anything she had ever imagined. They fueled her speculations on the meaning of all existence, her own included.

Fascination with natural history unexpectedly led to a major turning point in Mary Antin's life. On a natural history field trip she met Amadeus William Grabau (1870-1946), a geologist who had graduated from the Massachusetts Institute of Technology and was serving as a lecturer for the Boston Society of Natural History. Eleven years her senior, the handsome scientist was both the son and grandson of German-born Lutheran ministers and was completing his doctorate at Harvard University. The pair fell in love and were married in Boston on October 5, 1901.[7]

Marriage to Grabau took Mary Antin from Boston to New York, where her husband joined the faculty of Columbia University. There she fulfilled her dream of attending college, studying at Columbia's Teachers College (1901-02) and at Barnard College (1902-04), but without completing a degree. Antin initially warmed to her life as a faculty wife. Her husband's students found her a gracious hostess, and his position and her celebrity status won them both entree into New York intellectual society. And before too long the birth of the Grabaus' daughter, Josephine Esther, and motherhood completed the domestic portrait.[8]

Despite Antin's new roles as wife and mother, her ambitions for authorship did not wane. While most of her poetic efforts remained unpublished, Josephine Lazarus — a transcendentalist, sister of the poet Emma Lazarus, and a member of Antin's new circle of friends – convinced her to write her autobiography. The death of Lazarus in 1910 spurred her to begin the project. In September 1911 the *Atlantic Monthly* published "Malinke's Atonement," a short story Antin set in Polotzk about an impoverished nine-year-old and her testing of God.[9] Two months later the *Atlantic Monthly* published the first of several installments of what became her best known work, *The Promised Land* (1912).

In *The Promised Land,* a compelling story of deeply moving power, but lacking in the charming pubescent innocence displayed in her first book, Antin sketched her life in Polotzk and Boston. Espousing the myth of the American dream, she showed how the idea of America ran counter to the economic, political, and cultural oppression that she had known in Europe.[10] She pointed to her own adolescent success as proof of the abundant opportunities held out to immigrants who abandoned the old to embrace wholeheartedly the new. She also speculated grandly on the meaning of her own existence, concluding "that I am in the image of the universe, being myself; that I am the repository of all the wisdom in the world . . . The heir of the ages am I, and all that has been is in me, and shall continue to be in my immortal self." Extremely well received, *The Promised Land* sold nearly 85,000 copies before Antin's death and has since been reprinted several times.

The Promised Land brought Antin nationwide fame. She continued to write short stories for the *Atlantic* set in Polotzk or in immigrant neighborhoods, and she wrote opinion pieces for *The Outlook*.[11] In the same year that *The Promised Land* appeared, she campaigned for Theodore Roosevelt, who ran for president on the Progressive Party ticket. President

Roosevelt's friendship confirmed what Antin had for so long asserted—that nothing stood in the way of the immigrant in America. And Roosevelt revealed his debt to the immigrant when he wrote that he became a zealous supporter of women's suffrage precisely because of his association with women like Mary Antin.[12]

From 1913 to 1918 Antin traveled throughout the United States lecturing on civic and educational subjects. Her lectures were sponsored first by the Progressive Party, through the personal solicitation of Roosevelt, and later by the National Americanization Committee, the National Security League, and the U.S. Government Committee on Public Information. An eloquent and forceful speaker, Antin pleaded for liberty, democracy, and human rights in lectures on patriotism ("The Responsibility of American Citizenship," "How You and I Can Serve Our Country"); public education ("The Public School as a Test of American Faith"); Jewish immigrant life ("Jewish Life in the Pale: A Lesson for Americans," "Songs of the Ghetto"); and perhaps somewhat unexpectedly, Zionism ("The Zionist Movement").

The latter subject shows that despite her intermarriage, her ardent quest for Americanization, and her abandonment of the piety of the East European *shtetl,* she did not entirely cut herself off from Jewish life and thought. Even in *The Promised Land* she noted that her father had turned once again to Jewish tradition as he aged, and she wondered whether her grandchildren might someday discover that "the faith of Israel is a heritage that no heir in the direct line has the power to alienate from his successors." Perhaps her return visit to Polotzk after her marriage—a visit about which little is known—fueled these sentiments.

In "The Zionist Movement" Antin showed that while she still believed that the immigrant had to become Americanized, she had come to embrace Louis Brandeis' notion of Zionism as an Americanizing agent. Brandeis, the "people's attorney," Supreme Court Justice, and Zionist leader, argued that "To be a good American, one must be a good Jew, and to be a good Jew, one must be a good Zionist." Antin came to share this conviction. As America's immigration policy became increasingly restrictionist, it was becoming imperative to alleviate the suffering of persecuted Jews by reclaiming Palestine as the Jewish homeland. This noble effort in human rights, Antin insisted, deserved American support. In the same speech Antin also urged Jews to maintain those of their traditional values which offered larger social benefits. She apparently took her own words to heart, for she continued to celebrate some Jewish observances in her home.[13]

Despite her busy lecture schedule Antin continued to write. In 1914 she followed the success of *The Promised Land* with her last full-length work, *They Who Knock at Our Gates,* a polemic against the movement to restrict immigration. Although well received, this work was less popular than her autobiographical musings.

America's entry into World War I resulted in a serious personal crisis for Mary Antin—one which permanently changed her life. While she threw herself into lectures for the Allied cause ("America in the Light of the World War"), her husband, the son of a German immigrant and an admirer of German science, expressed his pro-German sympathies forcibly. This caused a severe rift in the Grabau household; husband and wife ceased to be on speaking terms. In 1918, fatigued and worried over her estrangement from her husband, Antin suffered an attack of what was then diagnosed as neurasthenia, and from which she never fully recovered. It caused her to retire from public life. Meanwhile, Grabau's pro-German sympathies made his situation at Columbia untenable. By 1919, when Grabau left Columbia, he and Antin had separated. The following year Grabau left for China to join the faculty of the National University at Peking. Although Antin and Grabau later resumed correspondence, illness and war kept her from visiting her husband in Peking, where he died on March 20, 1946.

After the Grabaus' separation, Antin left New York for Massachusetts. She divided her time between a social service community in Great Barrington known as the Gould farm, her family's home in Winchester, and her own apartment in Boston. She was hospitalized briefly and also worked as a hospital social worker. She continued during this period to wonder about the meaning of life, and was attracted by the concept of anthroposophy, propounded by Rudolph Steiner. In "The Soundless Trumpet," one of her very few late essays, she tried to convey the power of these new mystical insights—but without much success.

Her final years found Mary Antin mentally alert, but physically an invalid. She resided with her younger American-born sisters in their homes in Albany and New York City. She died of cancer on May 15, 1949 at the Pinehurst Nursing Home in Suffern, New York.

Numerous memoirs, histories, and novels recounting immigrant hardships have appeared since Mary Antin wrote *From Plotzk to Boston,* but few provide so detailed a picture of the physical journey from old world to new. Antin's depiction of her family's voyage, written within weeks of the event, permits the reader to enter, to imagine, and to remember a time when continents and oceans were seemingly insurmountable obstacles and when the journey from Europe to America required many weeks of exhausting travel by train, foot, and steamship. Thirteen-year-old Antin wrote a personal account, not a veiled brief for open immigration, like her later book, nor a self-serving autobiography like so many of this genre. Hers instead is a straightforward, honest account, written close to the events that she describes. Details might vary, but the trail *From Plotzk to Boston* would be reenacted by millions of immigrants — those who traveled from Berditchev to New York, from Warsaw to Philadelphia, from Odessa to Baltimore, and from hundreds of other European towns and villages bound for America.[15]

It was with enormous trepidation that the emigrants embarked upon this grand venture into the unknown. Carrying all their worldly possessions, they bid a tearful farewell to familiar places and faces and set off — destination "America." Like the unsung hero of Mary Antin's story — her mother — the emigrants had to cope with imposing gendarmes, wily agents, greedy hotel keepers, coarse sailors, impersonal physicians, and immigrant inspectors before they could shepherd their families safely to the new world. Along the way unexpected events often imperiled their journey. Each family's story was a saga unto itself.

The Antins' crisis came at the Russian-German border. Like the overwhelming majority of Russian Jews, they emigrated to America via Germany, armed with steerage-class tickets on one of the Reich's vast steamships. Because Imperial Russia technically did not allow emigration, most emigrants left Russia in stealth, following bands of smugglers who led them across the frontier under the cover of night. But the Antins were traveling in 1894 at a time when Germany, panicked by a cholera epidemic that it blamed on impoverished emigrants-in-transit, patrolled its frontier with great rigor. So the Antins, deciding not to risk an illegal crossing, procured passports to exit Russia openly. Unfortunately, they had not been warned that passports alone were insufficient for entry to Germany. To keep the poor and presumably most contagious travelers out of the Reich, German authorities were stopping all third-class passengers at the border and demanding that they upgrade to second-class if they wanted to get across. The Antins could not possibly manage five second-class fares. Only the intervention of a kindly German Jew, Herr Schidorsky, saved them from returning to Polotzk in despair.

Herr Schidorsky's generosity was but one example of the philanthropic activities that German Jews organized for their East European brethren in transit through Germany. As good citizens, German Jews naturally were expected to support the Reich's policy of deterring Jewish emigrants from settling in Germany. But nothing prevented them from offering those passing through en route to America, kosher food, clothing, shelter, and medical and legal assistance. Especially in the early years of mass migration many benefitted from this aid.

With the help of Herr Schidorsky, the Antins entered Germany. But the situation that caused their troubles had a lasting impact on the emigrants who followed them. Shipping lines needed an uninterrupted flow of East European emigrants to fill their huge steerage holds; they could not long absorb the losses brought on by German officials worried about the emigrants spreading disease. Only systematic control of the emigrants from the moment they crossed the frontier until they exited aboard a steamship bound for America could keep both the shipping companies and the German authorities happy.

In 1894, even as the Antins traveled through Germany, the development of this system of transmigrant control was in its final stages. Soon all emigrants would face the kind of examination and disinfection that had so frightened Mary Antin. Beginning in 1895, emigrants who crossed the frontier were taken to specially constructed border control stations where they were screened, bathed, and disinfected. They would leave the control stations only to travel, as the Antins had, locked inside special emigrant trains that sped from border to port so quickly that Germany was merely a blur of sky, earth, and buildings glimpsed through cracks in the siding. Arriving in either Bremen or Hamburg, the emigrants would then find themselves locked up once again to await the arrival of the ship that would carry them to freedom in the New World.

In Hamburg, the Antins were confined behind the high walls of the *Auswandererhallen*. Built by the Hamburg-Amerika Line in 1891, this emigrant hostel, which the Antins found dreary, crowded, and confining, did succeed in keeping the travelers off the city streets. Fortunately for later emigrants, within fifteen years massive emigration would cause the transformation of the *Auswandererhallen* into a cheery village of forty buildings, including a synagogue and kosher kitchen, capable of sheltering 4,000 people at a time. But for the Antins it was only another torment to suffer while anxiously awaiting the moment when they would, at last, be summoned to board ship.

The journey on board the *Polynesia* was the final hurdle and the worst. Crammed into the barnlike compartments which served those in steerage class as both sleeping and eating quarters, the Antins endured the noise and tumult and the rolling of the sea that brought with it the dreaded seasickness. What seemed like an eternity passed, ending eighteen days later, with a triumphant shout as the Antins joined their fellow travelers on deck for the joyful sight of land ahead. Sprucing themselves up as best they could after such a long ordeal, the travelers strained at the railing to catch a glimpse of that loved one – spouse, parent, sibling, child or cousin – whose face they had last seen years before. Formalities of landing and immigrant inspection had still to be endured, but they were not what they would be later at Ellis Island. It required only a short time before the way was cleared, allowing the immigrants to rush down the gangplank to those impatiently awaiting them. And so too did Mary Antin run, with arms open wide, to embrace her father – and America.

American University
Washington, October 1985

NOTES

----

[1]Polotzk, a city in the Lithuanian province of the Russian Empire, is today in the Belorussian U.S.S.R. When the Antins lived there, the 12,500 Jews of Polotzk comprised more than half its total population. In 1917 the Russian Revolution emancipated Soviet Jewry, and the Jews of Polotzk were at last free to leave the Pale of Settlement. Migration to Moscow and Leningrad and the death and dislocation brought on by World War I and the Russian Civil War caused its Jewish community to decline to some 8,000 men, women, and children by the eve of World War II. They were all murdered by the Nazis in December 1941. The printer of the first edition of *From Plotzk to Boston* mistakenly confused Antin's birthplace of Polotzk with the city of Plotzk, a city in the Warszawa province of central Poland (Plock in Polish). Antin corrected the error in her preface to the second edition, but let the title stand to avoid confusion; *Encyclopedia Judaica* vol. 13, (Jerusalem, 1972), cols. 647-48, 837.

[2]On Mary Antin, see the entry written by Oscar Handlin in *Notable American Women, 1607-1950: A Biographical Dictionary* vol. 1 (Cambridge, Mass., 1971), pp. 57-59; Handlin's introduction to the Sentry edition of Mary Antin's *The Promised Land* (1912, rpt. Boston: Houghton Mifflin Company, 1969); *The National Cyclopedia of American Biography* vol. 39, p. 40; *Who's Who in America* (1918-19), p. 98; *Who's Who in American Jewry* (1938-39), p. 33;

obituary in *The New York Times,* 18 May 1949, p. 27. The
history of her youth that follows is largely drawn from *The
Promised Land.*

[3] Mary's two youngest sisters, May and Celia, were born in
Boston.

[4] *The Promised Land,* pp. 204-205.

[5] Philip Cowen, *Memories of an American Jew* (1932; rpt. New
York, 1975), pp. 351-53; *From Plotzk to Boston* (Boston:
W.B. Clarke & Co., 1899).

[6] Antin was thirteen when she wrote *From Plotzk to Boston,*
not eleven, as Israel Zangwill claimed in his introduction
to the original edition.

[7] On Grabau, see Hervey W. Shimer, "Memorial to Amadeus
William Grabau," *Proceedings Volume of the Geological
Society of America, Annual Report for 1946,* pp. 155-66;
Wilhelm A. Grabau, *Die Geschichte der Familie Grabau*
(Leipzig, 1929), p. 188.

[8] Hervey Shimer, one of Grabau's students, recalled how Antin welcomed her husband's students to their small apartment; pp. 156-58. After the publication of *From Plotzk to
Boston* Antin spent her school holidays in New York at the
home of *American Hebrew* editor Philip Cowen and his
wife. During these vacations, the last of which took place
but a few months before her marriage, the Cowens intro-
duced her to their circle of friends, which included play-

wright Israel Zangwill, Yiddish poet Jessie Sampter, educator Rebecca Kohut, and artist Morris Rosenfeld. Presumably, these introductions facilitated her entry into New York intellectual society following her marriage and move; Cowen, pp. 353-387.

[9] *Atlantic Monthly* vol. 108 (September 1911), pp. 300-19.

[10] For a discussion of Antin and the myth of the American idea, see Sam B. Girgus, *The New Covenant: Jewish Writers and the American Idea* (Chapel Hill and London, 1984), pp. 5-6, 13-14.

[11] "The Amulet," *Atlantic Monthly* vol. 111 (January 1913), pp. 31-41; "The Lie," *Atlantic Monthly* vol. 112 (August 1913), pp. 177-90; "First Aid to the Alien," *The Outlook,* vol. 101 (29 June 1912), pp. 481-85.

[12] Mary Antin, "A Woman to Her Fellow-Citizens," *The Outlook* vol. 102 (2 November 1912), pp. 482-86; Theodore Roosevelt, "Chapters of a Possible Autobiography," *The Outlook,* vol. 104 (28 June 1913), pp. 472-6.

[13] On "The Zionist Idea," see a report of her address to the Alliance-Norma agricultural colony in New Jersey, in Joseph Brandes, *Immigrants to Freedom: Jewish Communities in Rural New Jersey since 1882* (Philadelphia, 1971), pp. 247-49. The Jewish Chautauquans there were so delighted with Antin's address that they renamed their group the Mary Antin Circle. Reform Rabbi Abraham Cronbach celebrated Chanukah with Antin and her

daughter (but without her husband) in the Grabaus' Scarsdale, New York home in 1916; "Autobiography," *American Jewish Archives* vol 11, no. 1 (April 1959), rpt. in Jacob R. Marcus, *Critical Studies in American Jewish History* vol. 3 (Cincinnati and New York, 1971), pp. 232-35. For a less attractive view of Antin and her Scarsdale home, see Ruth Rosen and Sue Davidson (eds.), *The Maimie Papers* (Westbury, New York, 1977), pp. 159-67.

[14] *Atlantic Monthly* vol. 159 (May 1937), pp. 560-69.

[15] Pamela S. Nadell, "The Journey to America by Steam: The Jews of Eastern Europe in Transition," *American Jewish History,* 71:2 (December 1981 pp. 269-284.

FOREWORD

The "infant phenomenon" in literature is rarer than in more physical branches of art, but its productions are not likely to be of value outside the doting domestic circle. Even Pope who "lisped in numbers for the numbers came," did not add to our Anthology from his cradle, though he may therein have acquired his monotonous rocking-metre. Immaturity of mind and experience, so easily disguised on the stage or the music-stool—even by adults—is more obvious in the field of pure intellect. The contribution with which Mary Antin makes her debut in letters is, however, saved from the emptiness of embryonic thinking by being a record of a real experience, the greatest of her life; her journey from Russia to Boston. Even so, and remarkable as her description is for a girl of eleven—for it was at this age that she first wrote the thing in Yiddish, though she was thirteen when she translated it into English—it would scarcely be worth publishing merely as a literary curiosity. But it happens to possess an extraneous value. For, despite the great wave of Russian immigration into the United States, and despite the noble spirit in which the Jews of

America have grappled with the invasion, we still know too little of the inner feelings of the people themselves, nor do we adequately realize what magic vision of free America lures them on to face the great journey to the other side of the world.

Mary Antin's vivid description of all she and her dear ones went through, enables us to see almost with our own eyes how the invasion of America appears to the impecunious invader. It is thus "a human document" of considerable value, as well as a promissory note of future performance. The quick senses of the child, her keen powers of observation and introspection, her impressionability both to sensations and complex emotions—these are the very things out of which literature is made; the raw stuff of art. Her capacity to handle English—after so short a residence in America—shows that she possesses also the instrument of expression. More fortunate than the poet of the Ghetto, Morris Rosenfeld, she will have at her command the most popular language in the world, and she has already produced in it passages of true literature, especially in her impressionistic rendering of the sea and the bustling phantasmagoria of travel.

What will be her development no one can say precisely, and I would not presume either to predict or to direct it, for "the wind bloweth where it listeth." It will probably take lyrical shape. Like most modern Jewesses who have written, she is, I fear, destined to spiritual suffering: fortunately her work evidences a genial talent for enjoyment and a warm humanity which may serve to counterbalance the curse of reflectiveness. That she is growing, is evident from her own Introduction, written only the other day, with its touches of humor and more complex manipulation of groups of facts. But I have ventured to counsel delay rather than precipitation in production—for she is not yet sixteen—and the completion of her education, physical no less than intellectual; and it is to this purpose that such profits as may accrue from this publication will be devoted. Let us hope this premature recognition of her potentialities will not injure their future flowering, and that her development will add to those spiritual and intellectual forces of which big-hearted American Judaism stands sorely in need. I should explain in conclusion, that I have neither added nor subtracted, even a comma, and that I have no credit in "discovering" Mary Antin. I did but endorse the verdict of that kind and charming Boston household in which I had the pleasure of encountering the gifted Russian girl, and to a member of which this little volume is appropriately dedicated.

I. ZANGWILL.

PREFATORY.

———

In the year 1891, a mighty wave of the emigration movement swept over all parts of Russia, carrying with it a vast number of the Jewish population to the distant shores of the New World—from tyranny to democracy, from darkness to light, from bondage and persecution to freedom, justice and equality. But the great mass knew nothing of these things; they were going to the foreign world in hopes only of earning their bread and worshiping their God in peace. The different currents that directed the course of that wave cannot be here enumerated. Suffice it to say that its power was enormous. All over the land homes were broken up, families separated, lives completely altered, for a common end.

The emigration fever was at its height in Polotzk, my native town, in the central western part of Russia, on the Dvina River. "America" was in everybody's mouth. Business men talked of it over their accounts; the market women made up their quarrels that they might discuss it from stall to stall; people who had relatives in the famous land went around reading their letters for the enlightenment of less fortunate folks; the one letter-carrier informed the public how many letters arrived from America, and who were the recipients; children played at emigrating; old folks shook their sage heads over the evening fire, and prophesied no good for those who braved the terrors of the sea and the foreign goal beyond it;—all talked of it, but scarcely anybody knew one true fact about this magic land. For book-knowledge was not for them; and a few persons—they were a dressmaker's daughter, and a merchant with his two sons—who had returned from America after a long visit, happened to be endowed with extraordinary imagination, (a faculty closely related to their knowledge of their old countrymen's ignorance), and their descriptions of life across the ocean, given daily, for some months, to eager audiences, surpassed anything in the Arabian Nights. One sad fact threw a shadow over the splendor of the gold-paved, Paradise-like fairyland. The travelers all agreed that Jews lived there in the most shocking impiety.

Driven by a necessity for bettering the family circumstances, and by certain minor forces which cannot now be named, my father began to think seriously of casting his lot with the great stream of emigrants. Many family councils were held before it was agreed that the plan must be carried out. Then came the parting; for it was impossible for the whole family to go at once. I remember it, though I was only eight. It struck me as rather interesting to stand on the platform before the train, with a crowd of friends weeping in sympathy with us, and father waving his hat for our special benefit, and saying—the last words we heard him speak as the train moved off—

"Good-bye, Polotzk, forever!"

Then followed three long years of hope and doubt for father in America and us in Russia. There were toil and suffering and waiting and anxiety for all. There were—but to tell of all that happened in those years I should have to write a separate history. The happy day came when we received the long-coveted summons. And what stirring times followed! The period of preparation was one of constant delight to us children. We were four—my two sisters, one brother and myself. Our playmates looked up to us in respectful admiration; neighbors, if they made no direct investigations, bribed us with nice things for information as to what was going into every box, package and basket. And the house was dismantled—people came and carried off the furniture; closets, sheds and other nooks were emptied of their contents; the great wood-pile was taken away until only a few logs remained; ancient treasures such as women are so loth to part with, and which mother had carried with her from a dear little house whence poverty had driven us, were brought to light from their hiding places, and sacrificed at the altar whose flames were consuming so much that was fraught with precious association and endeared by family tradition; the number of bundles and boxes increased daily, and our home vanished hourly;

the rooms became quite uninhabitable at last, and we children glanced in glee, to the anger of the echoes, when we heard that in the evening we were to start upon our journey.

But we did not go till the next morning, and then as secretly as possible. For, despite the glowing tales concerning America, people flocked to the departure of emigrants much as they did to a funeral; to weep and lament while (in the former case only, I believe) they envied. As everybody in Polotzk knew us, and as the departure of a whole family was very rousing, we dared not brave the sympathetic presence of the whole township, that we knew we might expect. So we gave out a false alarm.

Even then there was half the population of Polotzk on hand the next morning. We were the heroes of the hour. I remember how the women crowded around mother, charging her to deliver messages to their relatives in America; how they made the air ring with their unintelligible chorus; how they showered down upon us scores of suggestions and admonitions; how they made us frantic with their sympathetic weeping and wringing of hands; how, finally, the ringing of the signal bell set them all talking faster and louder than ever, in desperate efforts to give the last bits of advice, deliver the last messages, and, to their credit let it be said, to give the final, hearty, unfeigned good-bye kisses, hugs and good wishes.

Well, we lived through three years of waiting, and

also through a half hour of parting. Some of our relatives came near being carried off, as, heedless of the last bell, they lingered on in the car. But at last they, too, had to go, and we, the wanderers, could scarcely see the rainbow wave of colored handkerchiefs, as, dissolved in tears, we were carried out of Polotzk, away, from home, but nearer our longed-for haven of reunion; nearer, indeed, to everything that makes life beautiful and gives one an aim and an end—freedom, progress, knowledge, light and truth, with their glorious host of followers. But we did not know it then.

The following pages contain the description of our journey, as I wrote it four years ago, when it was all fresh in my memory. M. A.

Boston, January, 1899.

PREFACE TO SECOND EDITION.

I am glad of this opportunity to correct a mistake made in the first edition of this little sketch, which from the beginning had the good fortune of being put before a very considerable world of readers; namely, those of "The American Hebrew." A printer confounded the name of my native town, Polotzk, with that of the Polish town, Plotzk. Thus it happens that my birthplace is erroneously transferred to Poland, and even my friend Mr. Zangwill was sufficiently misled to call me a Polish girl; while, as a matter of fact, my native town is Polotzk, and I am consequently a Russian. While the necessary corrections have been made in the text, the title itself has been allowed to stand to avoid confusion.

I cannot let this excellent opportunity pass without making some acknowledgement of the many debts of gratitude I incurred through the publication of the story of my journey. To the world at large I owe many thanks for the warm kindness with which it received my little firstling. The ready, sympathetic appreciation which has met its entrance into a world usually critical enough has been such as to cause me no little surprise.

A few of the friends who did the most towards making the publication possible must be thanked individually. But for the repeated and urgent request of my dear friend once my teacher, Mary S. Dillingham, when I first knew her, now Mrs. Frederick Whiton, the little sketch would never have been translated into English. My friend to whom I gratefully dedicated the little volume was the first to suggest its publication and her untiring efforts brought me the friendly interest of Mr. Philip Cowen of "The American Hebrew," by whose unceasing kindness, together with that of Messrs. W. B. Clarke & Co., the publishers, the undertaking, which seemed to promise little enough success was carried through so well.

I believe that the warm welcome which met my little story is due more to the endorsement of my dear friend, Mr. Zangwill, than to any merits of the story itself. And I therefore take this opportunity of thanking the dear friend who has done so much for me,—so much!

M. A.

Boston, Mass., May 3, 1899.

FROM PLOTZK TO BOSTON.

———

The short journey from Polotzk to Vilna was uneventful. Station after station was passed without our taking any interest in anything, for that never-to-be-forgotten leave taking at the Plotzk railway station left us all in such a state of apathy to all things except our own thoughts as could not easily be thrown off. Indeed, had we not been obliged to change trains at Devinsk and, being the inexperienced travellers we were, do a great deal of bustling and hurrying and questioning of porters and mere idlers, I do not know how long we would have remained in that same thoughtful, silent state.

Towards evening we reached Vilna, and such a welcome as we got! Up to then I had never seen such a mob of porters and isvostchiky. I do not clearly remember just what occurred, but a most vivid recollection of being very uneasy for a time is still retained in my memory. You see my uncle was to have met us at the station, but urgent business kept him elsewhere.

Now it was universally believed in Polotzk that it was wise not to trust the first isvostchik who offered his services when one arrived in Vilna a stranger, and I do not

know to this day how mother managed to get away from
the mob, and how, above all, she dared to trust herself
with her precious baggage to one of them. But I have
thought better of Vilna isvostchiky since, for we were
safely landed after a pretty long drive in front of my uncle's store, with never one of our number lost, never
a bundle stolen or any mishap whatever.

Our stay in Vilna was marked by nothing of interest.
We stayed only long enough for some necessary papers
to reach us, and during that time I discovered that Vilna
was very much like Plotzk, though larger, cleaner and
noisier. There were the same coarse, hoarse-voiced
women in the market, the same kind of storekeepers in
the low store doors, forever struggling and quarrelling
for a customer. The only really interesting things I remember were the horsecars, which I had never even
heard of, and in one of which I had a lovely ride for five
copeiky, and a large book store on the Nemetzka yah
Ulitza. The latter object may not seem of any interest to
most people, but I had never seen so many books in one
place before, and I could not help regarding them with
longing and wonder.

At last all was in readiness for our start. This was
really the beginning of our long journey, which I shall
endeavor to describe.

I will not give any description of the various places we

passed, for we stopped at few places and always under circumstances which did not permit of sightseeing. I shall only speak of such things as made a distinct impression upon my mind, which, it must be remembered, was not mature enough to be impressed by what older minds were, while on the contrary it was in just the state to take in many things which others heeded not.

I do not know the exact date, but I do know that it was at the break of day on a Sunday and very early in April when we left Vilna. We had not slept any the night before. Fannie and I spent the long hours in playing various quiet games and watching the clock. At last the long expected hour arrived; our train would be due in a short time. All but Fannie and myself had by this time fallen into a drowse, half sitting, half lying on some of the many baskets and boxes that stood all about the room all ready to be taken to the station. So we set to work to rouse the rest, and with the aid of an alarm clock's loud ringing, we soon had them at least half awake; and while the others sat rubbing their eyes and trying to look wide awake, Uncle Borris had gone out, and when he returned with several droskies to convey us to the station, we were all ready for the start.

We went out into the street, and now I perceived that not we alone were sleepy; everything slept, and nature also slept, deeply, sweetly.

The sky was covered with dark gray clouds (perhaps that was its night-cap), from which a chill, drizzling rain was slowly descending, and the thick morning fog shut out the road from our sight. No sound came from any direction; slumber and quiet reigned everywhere, for every thing and person slept, forgetful for a time of joys, sorrows, hopes, fears,—everything.

Sleepily we said our last good-byes to the family, took our seats in the droskies, and soon the Hospitalnayah Ulitza was lost to sight. As the vehicles rattled along the deserted streets, the noise of the horses' hoofs and the wheels striking against the paving stones sounded unusually loud in the general hush, and caused the echoes to answer again and again from the silent streets and alleys.

In a short time we were at the station. In our impatience we had come too early, and now the waiting was very tiresome. Everybody knows how lively and noisy it is at a railroad station when a train is expected. But now there were but a few persons present, and in everybody's face I could see the reflection of my own dissatisfaction, because, like myself, they had much rather have been in a comfortable, warm bed than up and about in the rain and fog. Everything was so uncomfortable.

Suddenly we heard a long shrill whistle, to which the surrounding dreariness gave a strangely mournful sound, the clattering train rushed into the depot and stood still. Several passengers (they were very few) left the cars and hastened towards where the droskies stood, and after rousing the sleepy isvostchiky, were whirled away to their several destinations.

When we had secured our tickets and seen to the baggage we entered a car in the women's division and waited impatiently for the train to start. At last the first signal was given, then the second and third; the locomotive shrieked and puffed, the train moved slowly, then swiftly it left the depot far behind it.

From Vilna to our next stopping place, Verzbolovo, there was a long, tedious ride of about eight hours. As the day continued to be dull and foggy, very little could be seen through the windows. Besides, no one seemed to care or to be interested in anything. Sleepy and tired as we all were, we got little rest, except the younger ones, for we had not yet got used to living in the cars and could not make ourselves very comfortable. For the greater part of the time we remained as unsocial as the weather was unpleasant. The car was very still, there being few passengers, among them a very pleasant kind gentleman travelling with his pretty daughter. Mother found them very pleasant to chat with, and we children found it less tiresome to listen to them.

At half past twelve o'clock the train came to a stop before a large depot, and the conductor announced "Verzbolovo, fifteen minutes!" The sight that now presented itself was very cheering after our long, unpleasant ride. The weather had changed very much. The sun was shining brightly and not a trace of fog or cloud was to be seen. Crowds of well-dressed people were every-where—walking up and down the platform, passing through the many gates leading to the street, sitting around the long, well-loaded tables, eating, drinking, talking or reading newspapers, waited upon by the live-liest, busiest waiters I had ever seen—and there was such an activity and bustle about everything that I wished I could join in it, it seemed so hard to sit still. But I had to content myself with looking on with the others, while the friendly gentleman whose acquaintance my mother had made (I do not recollect his name) assisted her in ob-taining our tickets for Eidtkunen, and attending to every-thing else that needed attention, and there were many things.

Soon the fifteen minutes were up, our kind fellow-pas-senger and his daughter bade us farewell and a pleasant journey (we were just on the brink of the beginning of our troubles), the train puffed out of the depot and we all felt we were nearing a very important stage in our jour-ney. At this time, cholera was raging in Russia, and was spread by emigrants going to America in the coun-tries through which they travelled. To stop this danger, measures were taken to make emigration from Russia more difficult than ever. I believe that at all times the crossing of the boundary between Russia and Germany was a source of trouble to Russians, but with a special passport this was easily overcome. When, however, the traveller could not afford to supply himself with one, the boundary was crossed by stealth, and many amusing anecdotes are told of persons who crossed in some disguise, often that of a mujik who said he was going to the town on the German side to sell some goods, carried for the purpose of ensuring the success of the ruse. When several such tricks had been played on the guards it became very risky, and often, when caught, a traveller resorted to stratagem, which is very diverting when afterwards described, but not so at a time when much depends on its success. Some times a paltry bribe secured one a safe passage, and often emigrants were aided by men who made it their profession to help them cross, often suffering themselves to be paid such sums for the service that it paid best to be provided with a special passport.

As I said, the difficulties were greater at the time we were travelling, and our friends believed we had better not attempt a stealthy crossing, and we procured the necessary document to facilitate it. We therefore expected little trouble, but some we thought there might be, for we had heard some vague rumors to the effect that a special passport was not as powerful an agent as it used to be.

We now prepared to enjoy a little lunch, and before we had time to clear it away the train stopped, and we saw several men in blue uniforms, gilt buttons and brass helmets, if you may call them so, on their heads. At his side each wore a kind of leather case attached to a wide bronze belt. In these cases they carried something like a revolver, and each had, besides, a little book with black oil-cloth covers.

I can give you no idea of the impression these men (they were German gendarmes) made on us, by saying they frightened us. Perhaps because their (to us) impressive appearance gave them a stern look; perhaps because they really looked something more than grave, we were so frightened. I only know that we were. I can see the reason now clearly enough. Like all persons who were used to the tyranny of a Russian policeman, who practically ruled the ward or town under his friendly protection, and never hesitated to assert his rights as holder of unlimited authority over his little domain, in that mild, amiable manner so well known to such of his subjects as he particularly favored with his vigilant regard—like all such persons, I say, we did not, could not, expect to receive any kind treatment at the hands of a number of officers, especially as we were in the very act of attempting to part with our much-beloved mother country, of which act, to judge by the pains it took to make it difficult, the government did not approve. It was a natural fear in us, as you can easily see. Pretty soon mother recovered herself, and remembering that the train stops for a few minutes only, was beginning to put away the scattered articles hastily when a gendarme entered our car and said we were not to leave it. Mamma asked him why, but he said nothing and left the car, another gendarme entering as he did so. He demanded where we were going, and, hearing the answer, went out. Before we had had time to look about at each other's frightened faces, another man, a doctor, as we soon knew, came in followed by a third gendarme.

The doctor asked many questions about our health, and of what nationality we were. Then he asked about various things, as where we were going to, if we had tickets, how much money we had, where we came from, to whom we were going, etc., et·., making a note of every answer he received. This done, he shook his head with his shining helmet on it, and said slowly (I imagined he enjoyed frightening us), "With these third class tickets you cannot go to America now, because it is forbidden to admit emigrants into Germany who have not at least second class tickets. You will have to return to Russia unless you pay at the office here to have your tickets changed for second class ones." After a few minutes' calculation and reference to the notes he had made, he added calmly, "I find you will need two hundred rubles to get your tickets exchanged;" and, as the finishing stroke to his pleasing communication, added, "Your passports are of no use at all now because the necessary part has to be torn out, whether you are allowed to pass or not." A plain, short speech he made of it, that cruel man. Yet every word sounded in our ears with an awful sound that stopped the beating of our hearts for a while— sounded like the ringing of funeral bells to us, and yet without the mournfully sweet music those bells make, that they might heal while they hurt.

We were homeless, houseless, and friendless in a strange place. We had hardly money enough to last us through the voyage for which we had hoped and waited for three long years. We had suffered much that the reunion we longed for might come about; we had prepared ourselves to suffer more in order to bring it about, and had parted with those we loved, with places that were dear to us in spite of what we passed through in them, never again to see them, as we were convinced—all for the same dear end. With strong hopes and high spirits that hid the sad parting, we had started on our long journey. And now we were checked so unexpectedly but surely, the blow coming from where we little expected it, being, as we believed, safe in that quarter. And that is why the simple words had such a frightful meaning to us. We had received a wound we knew not how to heal.

When mother had recovered enough to speak she began to argue with the gendarme, telling him our story and begging him to be kind. The children were frightened by what they understood, and all but cried. I was only wondering what would happen, and wishing I could pour out my grief in tears, as the others did; but when I feel deeply I seldom show it in that way, and always wish I could.

Mother's supplications, and perhaps the children's indirect ones, had more effect than I supposed they would. The officer was moved, even if he had just said that tears would not be accepted instead of money, and gave us such kind advice that I began to be sorry I had thought him cruel, for it was easy to see that he was only doing his duty and had no part in our trouble that he could be blamed for, now that I had more kindly thoughts of him.

He said that we would now be taken to Keebart, a few versts' distance from Verzbolovo, where one Herr Schidorsky lived. This man, he said, was well known for miles around, and we were to tell him our story and ask him to help us, which he probably would, being very kind.

A ray of hope shone on each of the frightened faces listening so attentively to this bearer of both evil and happy tidings. I, for one, was very confident that the good man would help us through our difficulties, for I was most unwilling to believe that we really couldn't continue our journey. Which of us was? I'd like to know.

We are in Keebart, at the depot. The least important particular even of that place, I noticed and remembered. How the porter—he was an ugly, grinning man—carried in our things and put them away in the southern corner of the big room, on the floor: how we sat down on a settee near them, a yellow settee; how the glass roof let in so much light that we had to shade our eyes because the car had been dark and we had been crying; how there were only a few people besides ourselves there, and how I began to count them and stopped when I noticed a sign over the head of the fifth person—a little woman with a red nose and a pimple on it, that seemed to be staring at me as much as the grayish-blue eyes above them, it was so large and round—and tried to read the German, with the aid of the Russian translation below. I noticed all this and remembered it, as if there was nothing else in the world for me to think of—no America, no gendarme to destroy one's passports and speak of two hundred rubles as if he were a millionaire, no possibility of being sent back to one's old home whether one felt at all grateful for the kindness or not—nothing but that most attractive of places, full of interesting sights.

For, though I had been so hopeful a little while ago, I felt quite discouraged when a man, very sour and grumbling—and he was a Jew—a "Son of Mercy" as a certain song said—refused to tell mamma where Schidorsky lived. I then believed that the whole world must have united against us; and decided to show my defiant indifference by leaving the world to be as unkind as it pleased, while I took no interest in such trifles.

So I let my mind lose itself in a queer sort of mist—a something I cannot describe except by saying it must have been made up of lazy inactivity. Through this mist I saw and heard indistinctly much that followed.

When I think of it now, I see how selfish it was to allow myself to sink, body and mind, in such a sea of helpless laziness, when I might have done something besides awaiting the end of that critical time, whatever it might be—something, though what, I do not see even now, I own. But I only studied the many notices till I thought myself very well acquainted with the German tongue; and now and then tried to cheer the other children, who were still inclined to cry, by pointing out to them some of the things that interested me. For this faulty conduct I have no excuse to give, unless youth and the fact that I was stunned with the shock we had just received, will be accepted.

I remember through that mist that mother found Schidorsky's home at last, but was told she could not see him till a little later; that she came back to comfort us, and found there our former fellow passenger who had come with us from Vilna, and that he was very indignant at the way in which we were treated, and scolded, and declared he would have the matter in all the papers, and said we must be helped. I remember how mamma saw Schidorsky at last, spoke to him, and then told us, word for word, what his answer had been; that he wouldn't wait to be asked to use all his influence, and wouldn't lose a moment about it, and he didn't, for he went out at once on that errand, while his good daughter did her best to comfort mamma with kind words and tea. I remember that there was much going to the good man's house; much hurrying of special messengers to and from Eidtkunen; trembling inquiries, uncertain replies made hopeful only by the pitying, encouraging words and manners of the deliverer—for all, even the servants, were kind as good angels at that place. I remember that another little family—there were three—were discovered by us in the same happy state as ourselves, and like the dogs in the fable, who, receiving care at the hands of a kind man, sent their friends to him for help, we sent them to our helper.

I remember seeing night come out of that mist, and bringing more trains and people and noise than the whole day (we still remained at the depot), till I felt sick and dizzy. I remember wondering what kind of a night it was, but not knowing how to find out, as if I had no senses. I remember that somebody said we were obliged to remain in Keebart that night and that we set out to find lodgings; that the most important things I saw on the way were the two largest dolls I had ever seen, carried by two pretty little girls, and a big, handsome father; and a great deal of gravel in the streets, and boards for the crossings. I remember that we found a little room (we had to go up four steps first) that we could have for seventy-five copecks, with our tea paid for in that sum. I remember, through that mist, how I wondered what I was sleeping on that night, as I wondered about the weather; that we really woke up in the morning (I was so glad to rest I had believed we should never be disturbed again) and washed, and dressed and breakfasted and went to the depot again, to be always on hand. I remember that mamma and the father of the little family went at once to the only good man on earth (I thought so) and that the party of three were soon gone, by the help of some agent that was slower, for good reasons, in helping us.

I remember that mamma came to us soon after and

said that Herr Schidorsky had told her to ask the Postmeister—some high official there—for a pass to Eidtkunen; and there she should speak herself to our protector's
older brother who could help us by means of his great
power among the officers of high rank; that she returned
in a few hours and told us the two brothers were equal
in kindness, for the older one, too, said he would not wait
to be asked to do his best for us. I remember that another day—so-o-o long—passed behind the mist, and we
were still in that dreadful, noisy, tiresome depot, with no
change, till we went to spend the night at Herr Schidorsky's, because they wouldn't let us go anywhere else. On
the way there, I remember, I saw something marvellous
—queer little wooden sticks stuck on the lines where
clothes hung for some purpose. (I didn't think it was
for drying, because you know I always saw things hung
up on fences and gates for such purposes. The queer
things turned out to be clothes-pins). And, I remember,
I noticed many other things of equal importance to our
affairs, till we came to the little house in the garden.
Here we were received, I remember with much kindness
and hospitality. We had a fire made for us, food and
drink brought in, and a servant was always inquiring
whether anything more could be done for our comfort.

I remember, still through that misty veil, what a pleasant evening we passed, talking over what had so far hap-

pened, and wondering what would come. I must have talked like one lost in a thick fog, groping carefully. But, had I been shut up, mentally, in a tower nothing else could pierce, the sense of gratitude that naturally sprung from the kindness that surrounded us, must have, would have found a passage for itself to the deepest cavities of the heart. Yes, though all my senses were dulled by what had passed over us so lately, I was yet aware of the deepest sense of thankfulness one can ever feel. I was aware of something like the sweet presence of angels in the persons of good Schidorsky and his family. Oh, that some knowledge of that gratitude might reach those for whom we felt it so keenly! We all felt it. But the deepest emotions are so hard to express. I thought of this as I lay awake a little while, and said to myself, thinking of our benefactor, that he was a Jew, a true "Son of Mercy." And I slept with that thought. And this is the last I remember seeing and feeling behind that mist of lazy inactivity.

The next morning, I woke not only from the night's sleep, but from my waking dreaminess. All the vapors dispersed as I went into the pretty flower garden where the others were already at play, and by the time we had finished a good breakfast, served by a dear servant girl, I felt quite myself again.

Of course, mamma hastened to Herr Schidorsky as

soon as she could, and he sent her to the Postmeister again, to ask him to return the part of our passports that had been torn out, and without which we could not go on. He said he would return them as soon as he received word from Eidtkunen. So we could only wait and hope. At last it came and so suddenly that we ran off to the depot with hardly a hat on all our heads, or a coat on our backs, with two men running behind with our things, making it a very ridiculous sight. We have often laughed over it since.

Of course, in such a confusion we could not say even one word of farewell or thanks to our deliverers. But, turning to see that we were all there, I saw them standing in the gate, crying that all was well now, and wishing us many pleasant things, and looking as if they had been receiving all the blessings instead of us.

I have often thought they must have purposely arranged it that we should have to leave in a hurry, because they wouldn't stand any expression of gratefulness.

Well, we just reached our car in time to see our baggage brought from the office and ourselves inside, when the last bell rang. Then, before we could get breath enough to utter more than faint gasps of delight, we were again in Eidtkunen.

The gendarmes came to question us again, but when mother said that we were going to Herr Schidorsky of

Eidtkunen, as she had been told to say, we were allowed to leave the train. I really thought we were to be the visitors of the elder Schidorsky, but it turned out to be only an understanding between him and the officers that those claiming to be on their way to him were not to be troubled.

At any rate, we had now really crossed the forbidden boundary—we were in Germany.

There was a terrible confusion in the baggage-room where we were directed to go. Boxes, baskets, bags, valises, and great, shapeless things belonging to no particular class were thrown about by porters and other men, who sorted them and put tickets on all but those containing provisions, while others were opened and examined in haste. At last our turn came, and our things, along with those of all other American-bound travellers, were taken away to be steamed and smoked and other such processes gone through. We were told to wait till notice should be given us of something else to be done. Our train would not depart till nine in the evening.

As usual, I noticed all the little particulars of the waiting room. What else could I do with so much time and not even a book to read? I could describe it exactly— the large, square room, painted walls, long tables with fruits and drinks of all kinds covering them, the white chairs, carved settees, beautiful china and cut glass showing through the glass doors of the dressers, and the nickel samovar, which attracted my attention because I had never seen any but copper or brass ones. The best and the worst of everything there was a large case full of books. It was the best, because they were "books" and all could use them; the worst, because they were all German, and my studies in the railway depot of Keebart had not taught me so much that I should be able to read books in German. It was very hard to see people get those books and enjoy them while I couldn't. It was impossible to be content with other people's pleasure, and I wasn't.

When I had almost finished counting the books, I noticed that mamma and the others had made friends with a family of travellers like ourselves. Frau Gittleman and her five children made very interesting companions for the rest of the day, and they seemed to think that Frau Antin and the four younger Antins were just as interesting; perhaps excepting, in their minds, one of them who must have appeared rather uninteresting from a habit she had of looking about as if always expecting to make discoveries.

But she was interested, if not interesting, enough when the oldest of the young Gittlemans, who was a young gentleman of seventeen, produced some books which she could read. Then all had a merry time together, reading, talking, telling the various adventures of the journey, and walking, as far as we were allowed, up and down the long platform outside, till we were called to go and see, if we wanted to see, how our things were being made fit for further travel. It was interesting to see how they managed to have anything left to return to us, after all the processes of airing and smoking and steaming and other assaults on supposed germs of the dreaded cholera had been done with, the pillows, even, being ripped open to be steamed! All this was interesting, but we were rather disagreeably surprised when a bill for these unasked-for services had to be paid.

The Gittlemans, we found, were to keep us company for some time. At the expected hour we all tried to find room in a car indicated by the conductor. We tried, but could only find enough space on the floor for our baggage, on which we made believe sitting comfortably. For now we were obliged to exchange the comparative comforts of a third class passenger train for the certain discomforts of a fourth class one. There were only four narrow benches in the whole car, and about twice as many people were already seated on these as they were probably supposed to accommodate. All other space, to the last inch, was crowded by passengers or their luggage. It was very hot and close and altogether uncomfortable, and still at every new station fresh passengers came crowding in, and actually made room, spare as it was, for themselves. It became so terrible that all glared madly at the conductor as he allowed more people to come into that prison, and trembled at the announcement of every station. I cannot see even now how the officers could allow such a thing; it was really dangerous. The most remarkable thing was the good-nature of the poor passengers. Few showed a sour face even; not a man used any strong language (audibly, at least). They smiled at each other as if they meant to say, "I am having a good time; so are you, aren't you?" Young Gittleman was very gallant, and so cheerful that he attracted everybody's attention. He told stories, laughed, and made us unwilling to be outdone. During one of his narratives he produced a pretty memorandum book that pleased one of us very much, and that pleasing gentleman at once presented it to her. She has kept it since in memory of the giver, and, in the right place, I could tell more about that matter—very interesting.

I have given so much space to the description of that one night's adventures because I remember it so distinctly, with all its discomforts, and the contrast of our fellow-travellers' kindly dispositions. At length that dreadful night passed, and at dawn about half the passengers left, all at once. There was such a sigh of relief and a stretching of cramped limbs as can only be imagined, as the remaining passengers inhaled the fresh cold air of dewy dawn. It was almost worth the previous suffering to experience the pleasure of relief that followed.

All day long we travelled in the same train, sleeping, resting, eating, and wishing to get out. But the train stopped for a very short time at the many stations, and all the difference that made to us was that pretty girls passed through the cars with little bark baskets filled with fruit and flowers hardly fresher or prettier than their bearers, who generally sold something to our young companion, for he never wearied of entertaining us.

Other interests there were none. The scenery was nothing unusual, only towns, depots, roads, fields, little country houses with barns and cattle and poultry—all such as we were well acquainted with. If something new did appear, it was passed before one could get a good look at it. The most pleasing sights were little barefoot children waving their aprons or hats as we eagerly watched for them, because that reminded us of our doing the same thing when we saw the passenger trains, in the country. We used to wonder whether we should ever do so again.

Towards evening we came into Berlin. I grow dizzy even now when I think of our whirling through that city. It seemed we were going faster and faster all the time, but it was only the whirl of trains passing in opposite directions and close to us that made it seem so. The sight of crowds of people such as we had never seen before, hurrying to and fro, in and out of great depots that danced past us, helped to make it more so. Strange sights, splendid buildings, shops, people and animals, all mingled in one great, confused mass of a disposition to continually move in a great hurry, wildly, with no other aim but to make one's head go round and round, in following its dreadful motions. Round and round went my head. It was nothing but trains, depots, crowds—crowds, depots, trains, again and again, with no beginning, no end, only a mad dance! Faster and faster we go, faster still, and the noise increases with the speed. Bells, whistles, hammers, locomotives shrieking madly, men's voices, peddlers' cries, horses' hoofs, dogs' barking —all united in doing their best to drown every other sound but their own, and made such a deafening uproar in the attempt that nothing could keep it out. Whirl, noise, dance, uproar—will it last forever? I'm so—o diz-z-zy! How my head aches!

And oh! those people will be run over! Stop the train, they'll—thank goodness, nobody is hurt. But who ever heard of a train passing right through the middle of a city, up in the air, it seems. Oh, dear! it's no use thinking, my head spins so. Right through the business streets! Why, who ever—!

I must have lived through a century of this terrible motion and din and unheard of roads for trains, and confused thinking. But at length everything began to take a more familiar appearance again, the noise grew less, the roads more secluded, and by degrees we recognized the dear, peaceful country. Now we could think of Berlin, or rather, what we had seen of it, more calmly, and wonder why it made such an impression. I see now. We had never seen so large a city before, and were not prepared to see such sights, bursting upon us so suddenly as that. It was like allowing a blind man to see the full glare of the sun all at once. Our little Plotzk, and even the larger cities we had passed through, compared to Berlin about the same as total darkness does to great brilliancy of light.

In a great lonely field opposite a solitary wooden house within a large yard, our train pulled up at last, and a conductor commanded the passengers to make haste and get out. He need not have told us to hurry; we were glad enough to be free again after such a long imprisonment in the uncomfortable car. All rushed to the door. We breathed more freely in the open field, but the conductor did not wait for us to enjoy our freedom. He hurried us into the one large room which made up the house, and then into the yard. Here a great many men and women, dressed in white, received us, the women attending to the women and girls of the passengers, and the men to the others.

This was another scene of bewildering confusion, parents losing their children, and little ones crying; baggage being thrown together in one corner of the yard, heedless of contents, which suffered in consequence; those white-clad Germans shouting commands always accompanied with "Quick! Quick!"; the confused passengers obeying all orders like meek children, only questioning now and then what was going to be done with them.

And no wonder if in some minds stories arose of people being captured by robbers, murderers, and the like. Here we had been taken to a lonely place where only that house was to be seen; our things were taken away, our friends separated from us; a man came to inspect us, as if to ascertain our full value; strange looking people driving us about like dumb animals, helpless and unresisting; children we could not see, crying in a way that suggested terrible things; ourselves driven into a little room where a great kettle was boiling on a little stove; our clothes taken off, our bodies rubbed with a slippery substance that might be any bad thing; a shower of warm water let down on us without warning; again driven to another little room where we sit, wrapped in woollen blankets till large, coarse bags are brought in, their contents turned out and we see only a cloud of steam, and hear the women's orders to dress ourselves, quick, quick, or else we'll miss—something we cannot hear. We are forced to pick out our clothes from among all the others, with the steam blinding us; we choke, cough, entreat the women to give us time; they persist, "Quick, quick, or you'll miss the train!" Oh, so we really won't be murdered! They are only making us ready for the continuing of our journey, cleaning us of all suspicions of dangerous germs. Thank God!

Assured by the word "train" we manage to dress ourselves after a fashion, and the man comes again to inspect us. All is right, and we are allowed to go into the yard to find our friends and our luggage. Both are difficult tasks, the second even harder. Imagine all the things of some hundreds of people making a journey like ours, being mostly unpacked and mixed together in one sad heap. It was disheartening, but done at last was the task of collecting our belongings, and we were marched into the big room again. Here, on the bare floor, in a ring, sat some Polish men and women singing some hymn in their own tongue, and making more noise than music. We were obliged to stand and await further orders, the few seats being occupied, and the great door barred and locked. We were in a prison, and again felt some doubts. Then a man came in and called the passengers' names, and when they answered they were made to pay two

marcs each for the pleasant bath we had just been forced
to take.

Another half hour, and our train arrived. The door
was opened, and we rushed out into the field, glad to get
back even to the fourth class car.

We had lost sight of the Gittlemans, who were going a
different way now, and to our regret hadn't even said
good-bye, or thanked them for their kindness.

After the preceding night of wakefulness and discomfort, the weary day in the train, the dizzy whirl through
Berlin, the fright we had from the rough proceedings of
the Germans, and all the strange experiences of the place
we just escaped—after all this we needed rest. But to
get it was impossible for all but the youngest children. If
we had borne great discomforts on the night before, we
were suffering now. I had thought anything worse impossible. Worse it was now. The car was even more
crowded, and people gasped for breath. People sat in
strangers' laps, only glad of that. The floor was so
thickly lined that the conductor could not pass, and the
tickets were passed to him from hand to hand. To-night
all were more worn out, and that did not mend their dispositions. They could not help falling asleep and collid-
ing with someone's nodding head, which called out angry mutterings and growls. Some fell off their seats and
caused a great commotion by rolling over on the sleepers

on the floor, and, in spite of my own sleepiness and weariness, I had many quiet laughs by myself as I watched the
funny actions of the poor travellers.

Not until very late did I fall asleep. I, with the rest,
missed the pleasant company of our friends, the Gittlemans, and thought about them as I sat perched on a box,
with an old man's knees for the back of my seat, another man's head continually striking my right shoulder, a
dozen or so arms being tossed restlessly right in front of
my face, and as many legs holding me a fast prisoner,
so that I could only try to keep my seat against all the assaults of the sleepers who tried in vain to make their positions more comfortable. It was all so comical, in spite
of all the inconveniences, that I tried hard not to laugh
out loud, till I too fell asleep. I was awakened very early
in the morning by something chilling and uncomfortable
on my face, like raindrops coming down irregularly. I
found it was a neighbor of mine eating cheese, who was
dropping bits on my face. So I began the day with a
laugh at the man's funny apologies, but could not find
much more fun in the world on account of the cold and
the pain of every limb. It was very miserable, till some
breakfast cheered me up a little.

About eight o'clock we reached Hamburg. Again
there was a gendarme to ask questions, look over the
tickets and give directions. But all the time he kept a

distance from those passengers who came from Russia, all for fear of the cholera. We had noticed before how people were afraid to come near us, but since that memorable bath in Berlin, and all the steaming and smoking of our things, it seemed unnecessary.

We were marched up to the strangest sort of vehicle one could think of. It was a something I don't know any name for, though a little like an express wagon. At that time I had never seen such a high, narrow, long thing, so high that the women and girls couldn't climb up without the men's help, and great difficulty; so narrow that two persons could not sit comfortably side by side, and so long that it took me some time to move my eyes from the rear end, where the baggage was, to the front, where the driver sat.

When all had settled down at last (there were a number besides ourselves) the two horses started off very fast, in spite of their heavy load. Through noisy, strange looking streets they took us, where many people walked or ran or rode. Many splendid houses, stone and brick, and showy shops, they passed. Much that was very strange to us we saw, and little we knew anything about. There a little cart loaded with bottles or tin cans, drawn by a goat or a dog, sometimes two, attracted our attention. Sometimes it was only a nurse carrying a child in her arms that seemed interesting, from the strange dress. Often it was some article displayed in a shop window or door, or the usually smiling owner standing in the doorway, that called for our notice. Not that there was anything really unusual in many of these things, but a certain air of foreignness, which sometimes was very vague, surrounded everything that passed before our interested gaze as the horses hastened on.

The strangest sight of all we saw as we came into the still noisier streets. Something like a horse-car such as we had seen in Vilna for the first time, except that it was open on both sides (in most cases) but without any horses, came flying—really flying—past us. For we stared and looked it all over, and above, and under, and rubbed our eyes, and asked of one another what we saw, and nobody could find what it was that made the thing go. And go it did, one after another, faster than we, with nothing to move it. "Why, what that?" we kept exclaiming. "Really, do you see anything that makes it go? I'm sure I don't." Then I ventured the highly probable suggestion, "Perhaps it's the fat man in the gray coat and hat with silver buttons. I guess he pushes it. I've noticed one in front on every one of them, holding on to that shining thing." And I'm sure this was as wise a solution of the mystery as anyone could give, except the driver, who laughed to himself and his horses over our surprise and wonder at nothing he could see to cause it.

But we couldn't understand his explanation, though we always got along very easily with the Germans, and not until much later did we know that those wonderful things, with only a fat man to move them, were electric cars.

The sight-seeing was not all on our side. I noticed many people stopping to look at us as if amused, though most passed by as though used to such sights. We did make a queer appearance all in a long row, up above people's heads. In fact, we looked like a flock of giant fowls roosting, only wide awake.

Suddenly, when everything interesting seemed at an end, we all recollected how long it was since we had started on our funny ride. Hours, we thought, and still the horses ran. Now we rode through quieter streets where there were fewer shops and more wooden houses. Still the horses seemed to have but just started. I looked over our perch again. Something made me think of a description I had read of criminals being carried on long journeys in uncomfortable things—like this? Well, it was strange—this long, long drive, the conveyance, no word of explanation, and all, though going different ways, being packed off together. We were strangers; the driver knew it. He might take us anywhere—how could we tell? I was frightened again as in Berlin. The faces around me confessed the same.

The streets became quieter still; no shops, only little houses; hardly any people passing. Now we cross many railway tracks and I can hear the sea not very distant. There are many trees now by the roadside, and the wind whistles through their branches. The wheels and hoofs make a great noise on the stones, the roar of the sea and the wind among the branches have an unfriendly sound.

The horses never weary. Still they run. There are no houses now in view, save now and then a solitary one, far away. I can see the ocean. Oh, it is stormy. The dark waves roll inward, the white foam flies high in the air; deep sounds come from it. The wheels and hoofs make a great noise; the wind is stronger, and says, "Do you hear the sea?" And the ocean's roar threatens. The sea threatens, and the wind bids me hear it, and the hoofs and the wheels repeat the command, and so do the trees, by gestures.

Yes, we are frightened. We are very still. Some Polish women over there have fallen asleep, and the rest of us look such a picture of woe, and yet so funny, it is a sight to see and remember.

At last, at last! Those unwearied horses have stopped. Where? In front of a brick building, the only one on a large, broad street, where only the trees, and, in the distance, the passing trains can be seen. Nothing else. The ocean, too, is shut out.

All were helped off, the baggage put on the sidewalk, and then taken up again and carried into the building, where the passengers were ordered to go. On the left side of the little corridor was a small office where a man sat before a desk covered with papers. These he pushed aside when we entered, and called us in one by one, except, of course children. As usual, many questions were asked, the new ones being about our tickets. Then each person, children included, had to pay three marcs—one for the wagon that brought us over and two for food and lodgings, till our various ships should take us away.

Mamma, having five to pay for, owed fifteen marcs. The little sum we started with was to last us to the end of the journey, and would have done so if there hadn't been those unexpected bills to pay at Keebart, Eidtkunen, Berlin, and now at the office. Seeing how often services were forced upon us unasked and payment afterwards demanded, mother had begun to fear that we should need more money, and had sold some things to a woman for less than a third of their value. In spite of that, so heavy was the drain on the spare purse where it had not been expected, she found to her dismay that she had only twelve marcs left to meet the new bill.

The man in the office wouldn't believe it, and we were given over in charge of a woman in a dark gray dress and long white apron, with a red cross on her right arm. She led us away and thoroughly searched us all, as well as our baggage. That was nice treatment, like what we had been receiving since our first uninterrupted entrance into Germany. Always a call for money, always suspicion of our presence and always rough orders and scowls of disapproval, even at the quickest obedience. And now this outrageous indignity! We had to bear it all because we were going to America from a land cursed by the dreadful epidemic. Others besides ourselves shared these trials, the last one included, if that were any comfort, which it was not.

When the woman reported the result of the search as being fruitless, the man was satisfied, and we were ordered with the rest through many more examinations and ceremonies before we should be established under the quarantine, for that it was.

While waiting for our turn to be examined by the doctor I looked about, thinking it worth while to get acquainted with a place where we might be obliged to stay for I knew not how long. The room where we were sitting was large, with windows so high up that we couldn't see anything through them. In the middle stood several long wooden tables, and around these were settees of the same kind. On the right, opposite the doctor's office, was a little room where various things could be bought of a young man—if you hadn't paid all your money for other things.

When the doctor was through with us he told us to go to Number Five. Now wasn't that like in a prison? We walked up and down a long yard looking, among a row of low, numbered doors, for ours, when we heard an exclamation of, "Oh, Esther! how do you happen to be here?" and, on seeing the speaker, found it to be an old friend of ours from P lotzk. She had gone long before us, but her ship hadn't arrived yet. She was surprised to see us because we had had no intention of going when she went.

What a comfort it was to find a friend among all the strangers! She showed us at once to our new quarters, and while she talked to mamma I had time to see what they were like.

It looked something like a hospital, only less clean and comfortable; more like the soldiers' barracks I had seen. I saw a very large room, around whose walls were ranged rows of high iron double bedsteads, with coarse sacks stuffed with something like matting, and not over-clean blankets for the only bedding, except where people used their own. There were three windows almost touching the roof, with nails covering all the framework. From the ceiling hung two round gas lamps, and almost under them stood a little wooden table and a settee. The floor was of stone.

Here was a pleasant prospect. We had no idea how long this unattractive place might be our home.

Our friend explained that Number Five was only for Jewish women and girls, and the beds were sleeping rooms, dining rooms, parlors, and everything else, kitchens excepted. It seemed so, for some were lounging on the beds, some sitting up, some otherwise engaged, and all were talking and laughing and making a great noise. Poor things! there was nothing else to do in that prison.

Before mother had told our friend of our adventures, a girl, also a passenger, who had been walking in the yard, ran in and announced, "It's time to go to dinner! He has come already." "He" we soon learned, was the overseer of the Jewish special kitchen, without whom the meals were never taken.

All the inmates of Number Five rushed out in less than a minute, and I wondered why they hurried so. When we reached the place that served as dining room, there was hardly any room for us. Now, while the dinner is being served, I will tell you what I can see.

In the middle of the yard stood a number of long tables covered with white oilcloth. On either side of each table stood benches on which all the Jewish passengers were now seated, looking impatiently at the door with the sign "Jewish Kitchen" over it. Pretty soon a man appeared in the doorway, tall, spare, with a thin, pointed beard, and an air of importance on his face. It was "he", the overseer, who carried a large tin pail filled with black bread cut into pieces of half a pound each. He gave a piece to every person, the youngest child and the biggest man alike, and then went into the kitchen and filled his pail with soup and meat, giving everybody a great bowl full of soup and a small piece of meat. All attacked their rations as soon as they received them and greatly relished the coarse bread and dark, hot water they called soup. We couldn't eat those things and only wondered how any one could have such an appetite for such a dinner. We stopped wondering when our own little store of provisions gave out.

After dinner, the people went apart, some going back to their beds and others to walk in the yard or sit on the settees there. There was no other place to go to. The doors of the prison were never unlocked except when new passengers arrived or others left for their ships. The fences—they really were solid walls—had wires and nails on top, so that one couldn't even climb to get a look at the sea.

We went back to our quarters to talk over matters and rest from our journey. At six o'clock the doctor came with a clerk, and, standing before the door, bade all those in the yard belonging to Number Five assemble there; and then the roll was called and everybody received a little ticket as she answered to her name. With this all went to the kitchen and received two little rolls and a large cup of partly sweetened tea. This was supper; and breakfast, served too in this way was the same. Any wonder that people hurried to dinner and enjoyed it? And it was always the same thing, no change.

Little by little we became used to the new life, though it was hard to go hungry day after day, and bear the discomforts of the common room, shared by so many; the hard beds (we had little bedding of our own), and the confinement to the narrow limits of the yard, and the tiresome sameness of the life. Meal hours, of course, played the most important part, while the others had to be filled up as best we could. The weather was fine most of the time and that helped much. Everything was an event, the arrival of fresh passengers a great one which happened every day; the day when the women were allowed to wash clothes by the well was a holiday, and the few favorite girls who were allowed to help in the kitchen were envied. On dull, rainy days, the man coming to light the lamps at night was an object of pleasure, and every one made the best of everybody else. So when a young man arrived who had been to America once before, he was looked up to by every person there as a superior, his stories of our future home listened to with delight, and his manners imitated by all, as a sort of fit preparation. He was wanted everywhere, and he made the best of his greatness by taking liberties and putting on great airs and, I afterwards found, imposing on our ignorance very much. But anything "The American" did passed for good, except his going away a few days too soon.

Then a girl came who was rather wanting a little brightness. So all joined in imposing upon her by telling her a certain young man was a great professor whom all owed respect and homage to, and she would do anything in the world to express hers, while he used her to his best advantage, like the willing slave she was. Nobody seemed to think this unkind at all, and it really was excusable that the poor prisoners, hungry for some entertainment, should try to make a little fun when the chance came. Besides, the girl had opened the temptation by asking, "Who was the handsome man in the glasses? A professor surely;" showing that she took glasses for a sure sign of a professor, and professor for the highest possible title of honor. Doesn't this excuse us?

The greatest event was the arrival of some ship to take some of the waiting passengers. When the gates were opened and the lucky ones said good bye, those left behind felt hopeless of ever seeing the gates open for them. It was both pleasant and painful, for the strangers grew to be fast friends in a day and really rejoiced in each other's fortune, but the regretful envy could not be helped either.

Amid such events as these a day was like a month at least. Eight of these we had spent in quarantine when a great commotion was noticed among the people of Number Five and those of the corresponding number in the men's division. There was a good reason for it. You remember that it was April and Passover was coming on; in fact, it began that night. The great question was, Would we be able to keep it exactly according to the host of rules to be obeyed? You who know all about the great holiday can understand what the answer to that question meant to us. Think of all the work and care and money it takes to supply a family with all the things proper and necessary, and you will see that to supply a few hundred was no small matter. Now, were they going to take care that all was perfectly right, and could we trust them if they promised, or should we be forced to break any of the laws that ruled the holiday?

All day long there was talking and questioning and debating and threatening that "we would rather starve than touch anything we were not sure of." And we meant it. So some men and women went to the overseer to let him know what he had to look out for. He assured them that he would rather starve along with us than allow anything to be in the least wrong. Still, there was more discussing and shaking of heads, for they were not sure yet.

There was not a crumb anywhere to be found, because

what bread we received was too precious for any of it to be wasted; but the women made a great show of cleaning up Number Five, while they sighed and looked sad and told one another of the good hard times they had at home getting ready for Passover. Really, hard as it is, when one is used to it from childhood, it seems part of the holiday, and can't be left out. To sit down and wait for supper as on other nights seemed like breaking one of the laws. So they tried hard to be busy.

At night we were called by the overseer (who tried to look more important than ever in his holiday clothes—not his best, though) to the feast spread in one of the unoccupied rooms. We were ready for it, and anxious enough. We had had neither bread nor matzo for dinner, and were more hungry than ever, if that is possible. We now found everything really prepared; there were the pillows covered with a snow-white spread, new oilcloth on the newly scrubbed tables, some little candles stuck in a basin of sand on the window-sill for the women, and—a sure sign of a holiday—both gas lamps burning. Only one was used on other nights.

Happy to see these things, and smell the supper, we took our places and waited. Soon the cook came in and filled some glasses with wine from two bottles,—one yellow, one red. Then she gave to each person—exactly one and a half matzos; also some cold meat, burned almost to a coal for the occasion.

The young man—bless him—who had the honor to perform the ceremonies, was, fortunately for us all, one of the passengers. He felt for and with us, and it happened —just a coincidence—that the greater part of the ceremony escaped from his book as he turned the leaves. Though strictly religious, nobody felt in the least guilty about it, especially on account of the wine; for, when we came to the place where you have to drink the wine, we found it tasted like good vinegar, which made us all choke and gasp, and one little girl screamed "Poison!" so that all laughed, and the leader, who tried to go on, broke down too at the sight of the wry faces he saw; while the overseer looked shocked, the cook nearly set her gown on fire by overthrowing the candles with her apron(used to hide her face) and all wished our Master Overseer had to drink that "wine" all his days.

Think of the same ceremony as it is at home, then of this one just described. Do they even resemble each other?

Well, the leader got through amid much giggling and sly looks among the girls who understood the trick, and frowns of the older people (who secretly blessed him for it). Then, half hungry, all went to bed and dreamed of food in plenty.

No other dreams? Rather! For the day that brought the Passover brought us—our own family—the most glorious news. We had been ordered to bring our baggage to the office!

"Ordered to bring our baggage to the office!" That meant nothing less than that we were "going the next day!"

It was just after supper that we received the welcome order. Oh, who cared if there wasn't enough to eat? Who cared for anything in the whole world? We didn't. It was all joy and gladness and happy anticipation for us. We laughed, and cried, and hugged one another, and shouted, and acted altogether like wild things. Yes, we were wild with joy, and long after the rest were asleep, we were whispering together and wondering how we could keep quiet the whole night. We couldn't sleep by any means, we were so afraid of oversleeping the great hour; and every little while, after we tried to sleep, one of us would suddenly think she saw day at the window, and wake the rest, who also had only been pretending to sleep while watching in the dark for daylight.

When it came, it found no watchful eye, after all. The excitement gave way to fatigue, and drowsiness first, then deep sleep, completed its victory. It was eight o'clock when we awoke. The morning was cloudy and chilly, the sun being too lazy to attend to business; now and then it rained a little, too. And yet it was the most beautiful day that had ever dawned on Hamburg.

We enjoyed everything offered for breakfast, two mat-zos and two cups of tea apiece—why it was a banquet. After it came the good-byes, as we were going soon. As I told you before, the strangers became fast friends in a short time under the circumstances, so there was real sorrow at the partings, though the joy of the fortunate ones was, in a measure, shared by all.

About one o'clock (we didn't go to dinner—we couldn't eat for excitement) we were called. There were three other families, an old woman, and a young man, among the Jewish passengers, who were going with us, besides some Polish people. We were all hurried through the door we had watched with longing for so long, and were a little way from it when the old woman stopped short and called on the rest to wait.

"We haven't any matzo!" she cried in alarm. "Where's the overseer?"

Sure enough we had forgotten it, when we might as well have left one of us behind. We refused to go, calling for the overseer, who had promised to supply us, and the man who had us in charge grew angry and said he wouldn't wait. It was a terrible situation for us.

"Oh," said the man, "you can go and get your matzo, but the boat won't wait for you." And he walked off, followed by the Polish people only.

We had to decide at once. We looked at the old woman. She said she wasn't going to start on a dangerous journey with such a sin on her soul. Then the children decided. They understood the matter. They cried and begged to follow the party. And we did.

Just when we reached the shore, the cook came up panting hard. She brought us matzo. How relieved we were then!

We got on a little steamer (the name is too big for it) that was managed by our conductor alone. Before we had recovered from the shock of the shrill whistle so near us, we were landing in front of a large stone building.

Once more we were under the command of the gendarme. We were ordered to go into a big room crowded with people, and wait till the name of our ship was called. Somebody in a little room called a great many queer names, and many passengers answered the call. At last we heard, "Polynesia!"

We passed in and a great many things were done to our tickets before we were directed to go outside, then to a larger steamer than the one we came in. At every step our tickets were either stamped or punched, or a piece torn off of them, till we stepped upon the steamer's deck. Then we were ordered below. It was dark there, and we didn't like it. In a little while we were called up again, and then we saw before us the great ship that was to carry us to America.

I only remember, from that moment, that I had only one care till all became quiet; not to lose hold of my sister's hand. Everything else can be told in one word— noise. But when I look back, I can see what made it. There were sailors dragging and hauling bundles and boxes from the small boat into the great ship, shouting and thundering at their work. There were officers giving out orders in loud voices, like trumpets, though they seemed to make no effort. There were children crying, and mothers hushing them, and fathers questioning the officers as to where they should go. There were little boats and steamers passing all around, shrieking and whistling terribly. And there seemed to be everything under heaven that had any noise in it, come to help swell the confusion of sounds. I know that, but how we ever got in that quiet place that had the sign "For Families" over it, I don't know. I think we went around and around, long and far, before we got there.

But there we were, sitting quietly on a bench by the white berths.

When the sailors brought our things, we got everything in order for the journey as soon as possible, that we might go on deck to see the starting. But first we had to obey a sailor, who told us to come and get dishes. Each person received a plate, a spoon and a cup. I wondered how we could get along if we had had no things of our own.

For an hour or two more there were still many noises on deck, and many preparations made. Then we went up, as most of the passengers did.

What a change in the scene! Where there had been noise and confusion before, peace and quiet were now. All the little boats and steamers had disappeared, and the wharf was deserted. On deck the "Polynesia" everything was in good order, and the officers walked about smoking their cigars as if their work was done. Only a few sailors were at work at the big ropes, but they didn't shout as before. The weather had changed, too, for the twilight was unlike what the day had promised. The sky was soft gray, with faint streaks of yellow on the horizon. The air was still and pleasant, much warmer than it had been all the day; and the water was as motionless and clear as a deep, cool well, and everything was mirrored in it clearly.

This entire change in the scene, the peace that encircled everything around us, seemed to give all the same feeling that I know I had. I fancied that nature created it especially for us, so that we would be allowed, in this pause, to think of our situation. All seemed to do so; all spoke in low voices, and seemed to be looking for something as they gazed quietly into the smooth depths below, or the twilight skies above. Were they seeking an assurance? Perhaps; for there was something strange in the absence of a crowd of friends on the shore, to cheer and salute, and fill the air with white clouds and last farewells.

I found the assurance. The very stillness was a voice —nature's voice; and it spoke to the ocean and said,

"I entrust to you this vessel. Take care of it, for it bears my children with it, from one strange shore to another more distant, where loving friends are waiting to embrace them after long partings. Be gentle with your charge."

And the ocean, though seeming so still, replied,

"I will obey my mistress."

I heard it all, and a feeling of safety and protection came to me. And when at last the wheels overhead began to turn and clatter, and the ripples on the water told us that the "Polynesia" had started on her journey, which was not noticeable from any other sign, I felt only a sense of happiness. I mistrusted nothing.

But the old woman who remembered the matzo did, more than anybody else. She made great preparations for being seasick, and poisoned the air with garlic and onions.

When the lantern fixed in the ceiling had been lighted, the captain and the steward paid us a visit. They took up our tickets and noticed all the passengers, then left. Then a sailor brought supper—bread and coffee. Only a few ate it. Then all went to bed, though it was very early.

Nobody expected seasickness as soon as it seized us. All slept quietly the whole night, not knowing any difference between being on land or at sea. About five o'clock I woke up, and then I felt and heard the sea. A very disagreeable smell came from it, and I knew it was disturbed by the rocking of the ship. Oh, how wretched it made us! From side to side it went rocking, rocking. Ugh! Many of the passengers are very sick indeed, they suffer terribly. We are all awake now, and wonder if we, too, will be so sick. Some children are crying, at intervals. There is nobody to comfort them—all are so miserable. Oh, I am so sick! I'm dizzy; everything is going round and round before my eyes—Oh-h-h!

I can't even begin to tell of the suffering of the next few hours. Then I thought I would feel better if I could go on deck. Somehow, I got down (we had upper berths) and, supporting myself against the walls, I came on deck. But it was worse. The green water, tossing up the white foam, rocking all around, as far as I dared to look, was frightful to me then. So I crawled back as well as I could, and nobody else tried to go out.

By and by the doctor and the steward came. The doctor asked each passenger if they were well, but only smiled when all begged for some medicine to take away the dreadful suffering. To those who suffered from anything besides seasickness he sent medicine and special food later on. His companion appointed one of the men passengers for every twelve or fifteen to carry the meals from the kitchen, giving them cards to get it with. For our group a young German was appointed, who was making the journey for the second time, with his mother and sister. We were great friends with them during the journey.

The doctor went away soon, leaving the sufferers in the same sad condition. At twelve, a sailor announced that dinner was ready, and the man brought it—large tin pails and basins of soup, meat, cabbage, potatoes, and pudding (the last was allowed only once a week); and almost all of it was thrown away, as only a few men ate. The rest couldn't bear even the smell of food. It was the same with the supper at six o'clock. At three milk had been brought for the babies, and brown bread (a treat) with coffee for the rest. But after supper the daily allowance of fresh water was brought, and this soon disappeared and more called for, which was refused, although we lived on water alone for a week.

At last the day was gone, and much we had borne in it. Night came, but brought little relief. Some did fall asleep, and forgot suffering for a few hours. I was awake late. The ship was quieter, and everything sadder than by daylight. I thought of all we had gone through till we had got on board the "Polynesia"; of the parting from all friends and things we loved, forever, as far as we knew; of the strange experience at various strange places; of the kind friends who helped us, and the rough officers who commanded us; of the quarantine, the hunger, then the happy news, and the coming on board. Of all this I thought, and remembered that we were far away from friends, and longed for them, that I might be made well by speaking to them. And every minute was making the distance between us greater, a meeting more impossible. Then I remembered why we were crossing the ocean, and knew that it was worth the price. At last the noise of the wheels overhead, and the dull roar of the sea, rocked me to sleep.

For a short time only. The ship was tossed about more than the day before, and the great waves sounded like distant thunder as they beat against it, and rolled across the deck and entered the cabin. We found, however, that we were better, though very weak. We managed to go on deck in the afternoon, when it was calm enough. A little band was playing, and a few young sailors and German girls tried even to dance; but it was impossible.

As I sat in a corner where no waves could reach me, holding on to a rope, I tried to take in the grand scene. There was the mighty ocean I had heard of only, spreading out its rough breadth far, far around, its waves giving out deep, angry tones, and throwing up walls of spray into the air. There was the sky, like the sea, full of ridges of darkest clouds, bending to meet the waves, and following their motions and frowning and threatening. And there was the "Polynesia" in the midst of this world of gloom, and anger, and distance. I saw these, but indistinctly, not half comprehending the wonderful picture. For the suffering had left me dull and tired out. I only knew that I was sad, and everybody else was the same.

Another day gone, and we congratulate one another that seasickness lasted only one day with us. So we go to sleep.

Oh, the sad mistake! For six days longer we remain in our berths, miserable and unable to eat. It is a long fast, hardly interrupted, during which we know that the weather is unchanged, the sky dark, the sea stormy.

On the eighth day out we are again able to be about. I went around everywhere, exploring every corner, and learning much from the sailors; but I never remembered the names of the various things I asked about, they were so many, and some German names hard to learn. We all made friends with the captain and other officers, and many of the passengers. The little band played regularly on certain days, and the sailors and girls had a good many dances, though often they were swept by a wave across the deck, quite out of time. The children were allowed to play on deck, but carefully watched.

Still the weather continued the same, or changing slightly. But I was able now to see all the grandeur of my surroundings, notwithstanding the weather.

Oh, what solemn thoughts I had! How deeply I felt the greatness, the power of the scene! The immeasurable distance from horizon to horizon; the huge billows forever changing their shapes—now only a wavy and rolling plain, now a chain of great mountains, coming and going farther away; then a town in the distance, perhaps, with spires and towers and buildings of gigantic dimensions; and mostly a vast mass of uncertain shapes, knocking against each other in fury, and seething and foaming in their anger; the grey sky, with its mountains of gloomy clouds, flying, moving with the waves, as it seemed, very near them; the absence of any object besides the one ship; and the deep, solemn groans of the sea, sounding as if all the voices of the world had been turned into sighs and then gathered into that one mournful sound—so deeply did I feel the presence of these things, that the feeling became one of awe, both painful and sweet, and stirring and warming, and deep and calm and grand.

I thought of tempests and shipwreck, of lives lost, treasures destroyed, and all the tales I had heard of the misfortunes at sea, and knew I had never before had such a clear idea of them. I tried to realize that I saw only a part of an immense whole, and then my feelings were terrible in their force. I was afraid of thinking then, but could not stop it. My mind would go on working, till I was overcome by the strength and power that was greater than myself. What I did at such times I do not know. I must have been dazed.

After a while I could sit quietly and gaze far away. Then I would imagine myself all alone on the ocean, and Robinson Crusoe was very real to me. I was alone sometimes. I was aware of no human presence; I was conscious only of sea and sky and something I did not understand. And as I listened to its solemn voice, I felt as if I had found a friend, and knew that I loved the ocean. It seemed as if it were within as well as without, a part of myself; and I wondered how I had lived without it, and if I could ever part with it.

The ocean spoke to me in other besides mournful or angry tones. I loved even the angry voice, but when it became soothing, I could hear a sweet, gentle accent that reached my soul rather than my ear. Perhaps I imagined it. I do not know. What was real and what imaginary blended in one. But I heard and felt it, and at such moments I wished I could live on the sea forever, and thought that the sight of land would be very unwelcome to me. I did not want to be near any person. Alone with the ocean forever—that was my wish.

Leading a quiet life, the same every day, and thinking such thoughts, feeling such emotions, the days were very long. I do not know how the others passed the time, because I was so lost in my meditations. But when the sky would smile for awhile—when a little sunlight broke a path for itself through the heavy clouds, which disappeared as though frightened; and when the sea looked more friendly, and changed its color to match the heavens, which were higher up—then we would sit on deck together, and laugh for mere happiness as we talked of the nearing meeting, which the unusual fairness of the weather seemed to bring nearer. Sometimes, at such minutes of sunshine and gladness, a few birds would be seen making their swift journey to some point we did not know of; sometimes among the light clouds, then almost touching the surface of the waves. How shall I tell you what we felt at the sight? The birds were like old friends to us, and brought back many memories, which seemed very old, though really fresh. All felt sadder when the distance became too great for us to see the dear little friends, though it was not for a long time after their first appearance. We used to watch for them, and often mistook the clouds for birds, and were thus disappointed. When they did come, how envious we were of their wings! It was a new thought to me that the birds had more power than man.

In this way the days went by. I thought my thoughts each day, as I watched the scene, hoping to see a beautiful sunset some day. I never did, to my disappointment. And each night, as I lay in my berth, waiting for sleep, I wished I might be able even to hope for the happiness of a sea-voyage after this had been ended.

Yet, when, on the twelfth day after leaving Hamburg, the captain announced that we should see land before long, I rejoiced as much as anybody else. We were so excited with expectation that nothing else was heard but the talk of the happy arrival, now so near. Some were even willing to stay up at night, to be the first ones to see the shores of America. It was therefore a great disappointment when the captain said, in the evening, that we would not reach Boston as soon as he expected, on account of the weather.

A dense fog set in at night, and grew heavier and heavier, until the "Polynesia" was closely walled in by it, and we could just see from one end of the deck to the other. The signal lanterns were put up, the passengers were driven to their berths by the cold and damp, the cabin doors closed, and discomfort reigned everywhere.

But the excitement of the day had tired us out, and we were glad to forget disappointment in sleep. In the morning it was still foggy, but we could see a little way around. It was very strange to have the boundless distance made so narrow, and I felt the strangeness of the scene. All day long we shivered with cold, and hardly left the cabin. At last it was night once more, and we in our berths. But nobody slept.

The sea had been growing rougher during the day, and at night the ship began to pitch as it did at the beginning of the journey. Then it grew worse. Everything in our cabin was rolling on the floor, clattering and dinning. Dishes were broken into little bits that flew about from one end to the other. Bedding from upper berths nearly stifled the people in the lower ones. Some fell out of their berths, but it was not at all funny. As the ship turned to one side, the passengers were violently thrown against that side of the berths, and some boards gave way and clattered down to the floor. When it tossed on the other side, we could see the little windows almost touch the water, and closed the shutters to keep out the sight. The children cried, everybody groaned, and sailors kept coming in to pick up the things on the floor and carry them away. This made the confusion less, but not the alarm.

Above all sounds rose the fog horn. It never stopped the long night through. And oh, how sad it sounded! It pierced every heart, and made us afraid. Now and then some ship, far away, would answer, like a weak echo. Sometimes we noticed that the wheels were still, and we knew that the ship had stopped. This frightened us more than ever, for we imagined the worst reasons for it.

It was day again, and a little calmer. We slept now, till the afternoon. Then we saw that the fog had become much thinner, and later on we even saw a ship, but indistinctly.

Another night passed, and the day that followed was pretty fair, and towards evening the sky was almost cloudless. The captain said we should have no more rough weather, for now we were really near Boston. Oh, how hard it was to wait for the happy day! Somebody brought the news that we should land to-morrow in the afternoon. We didn't believe it, so he said that the steward had ordered a great pudding full of raisins for supper that day as a sure sign that it was the last on board. We remembered the pudding, but didn't believe in its meaning.

I don't think we slept that night. After all the suffering of our journey, after seeing and hearing nothing but the sky and the sea and its roaring, it was impossible to sleep when we thought that soon we would see trees, fields, fresh people, animals—a world, and that world America. Then, above everything, was the meeting with friends we had not seen for years; for almost everybody had some friend awaiting them.

Morning found all the passengers up and expectant.

Someone questioned the captain, and he said we would land to-morrow. There was another long day, and another sleepless night, but when these ended at last, how busy we were! First we packed up all the things we did not need, then put on fresh clothing, and then went on deck to watch for land. It was almost three o'clock, the hour the captain hoped to reach Boston, but there was nothing new to be seen. The weather was fair, so we would have seen anything within a number of miles. Anxiously we watched, and as we talked of the strange delay, our courage began to give out with our hope. When it could be borne no longer, a gentleman went to speak to the captain. He was on the upper deck, examining the horizon. He put off the arrival for the next day!

You can imagine our feelings at this. When it was worse the captain came down and talked so assuringly that, in spite of all the disappointments we had had, we believed that this was the last, and were quite cheerful when we went to bed.

The morning was glorious. It was the eighth of May, the seventeenth day after we left Hamburg. The sky was clear and blue, the sun shone brightly, as if to congratulate us that we had safely crossed the stormy sea, and to apologize for having kept away from us so long. The sea had lost its fury; it was almost as quiet as it had been at Hamburg before we started, and its color was a beautiful greenish blue. Birds were all the time in the air, and it was worth while to live merely to hear their songs. And soon, oh joyful sight! we saw the tops of two trees!

What a shout there rose! Everyone pointed out the welcome sight to everybody else, as if they did not see it. All eyes were fixed on it as if they saw a miracle. And this was only the beginning of the joys of the day!

What confusion there was! Some were flying up the stairs to the upper deck, some were tearing down to the lower one, others were running in and out of the cabins, some were in all parts of the ship in one minute, and all were talking and laughing and getting in somebody's way. Such excitement, such joy! We had seen two trees!

Then steamers and boats of all kinds passed by, in all directions. We shouted, and the men stood up in the boats and returned the greeting, waving their hats. We were as glad to see them as if they were old friends of ours.

Oh, what a beautiful scene! No corner of the earth is half so fair as the lovely picture before us. It came to view suddenly,—a green field, a real field with grass on it, and large houses, and the dearest hens and little chickens in all the world, and trees, and birds, and people at work.

The young green things put new life into us, and are so dear to our eyes that we dare not speak a word now, lest the magic should vanish away and we should be left to the stormy scenes we know.

But nothing disturbed the fairy sight. Instead, new scenes appeared, beautiful as the first. The sky becomes bluer all the time, the sun warmer; the sea is too quiet for its name, and the most beautiful blue imaginable.

What are the feelings these sights awaken! They can not be described. To know how great was our happiness, how complete, how free from even the shadow of a sadness, you must make a journey of sixteen days on a stormy ocean. Is it possible that we will ever again be so happy?

It was about three hours since we saw the first landmarks, when a number of men came on board, from a little steamer, and examined the passengers to see if they were properly vaccinated (we had been vaccinated on the "Polynesia"), and pronounced everyone all right. Then they went away, except one man who remained. An hour later we saw the wharves.

Before the ship had fully stopped, the climax of our joy was reached. One of us espied the figure and face we had longed to see for three long years. In a moment five passengers on the "Polynesia" were crying, "Papa," and gesticulating, and laughing, and hugging one another, and going wild altogether. All the rest were roused by our excitement, and came to see our father. He recognized us as soon as we him, and stood apart on the wharf not knowing what to do, I thought.

What followed was slow torture. Like mad things we ran about where there was room, unable to stand still as long as we were on the ship and he on shore. To have crossed the ocean only to come within a few yards of him, unable to get nearer till all the fuss was over, was dreadful enough. But to hear other passengers called who had no reason for hurry, while we were left among the last, was unendurable.

Oh, dear! Why can't we get off the hateful ship? Why can't papa come to us? Why so many ceremonies at the landing?

We said goodbye to our friends as their turn came, wishing we were in their luck. To give us something else to think of, papa succeeded in passing us some fruit; and we wondered to find it anything but a great wonder, for we expected to find everything marvellous in the strange country.

Still the ceremonies went on. Each person was asked a hundred or so stupid questions, and all their answers were written down by a very slow man. The baggage had to be examined, the tickets, and a hundred other things done before anyone was allowed to step ashore, all to keep us back as long as possible.

Now imagine yourself parting with all you love, believing it to be a parting for life; breaking up your home, selling the things that years have made dear to you; starting on a journey without the least experience in travelling, in the face of many inconveniences on account of the want of sufficient money; being met with disappointment where it was not to be expected; with rough treatment everywhere, till you are forced to go and make friends for yourself among strangers; being obliged to sell some of your most necessary things to pay bills you did not willingly incur; being mistrusted and searched, then half starved, and lodged in common with a multitude of strangers; suffering the miseries of seasickness, the disturbances and alarms of a stormy sea for sixteen days; and then stand within a few yards of him for whom you did all this, unable to even speak to him easily. How do you feel?

Oh, it's our turn at last! We are questioned, examined, and dismissed! A rush over the planks on one side, over the ground on the other, six wild beings cling to each other, bound by a common bond of tender joy, and the long parting is at an END.

Drawing
WHALES & DOLPHINS
A STEP-BY-STEP FUN GUIDE

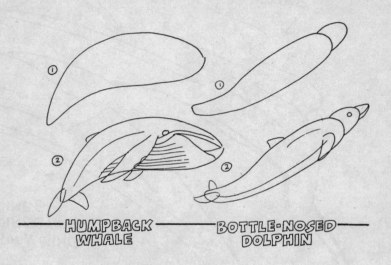

HUMPBACK WHALE

BOTTLE-NOSED DOLPHIN

Published by: **Watermill Press**
Mahwah, New Jersey
ISBN 0-8167-1670-6

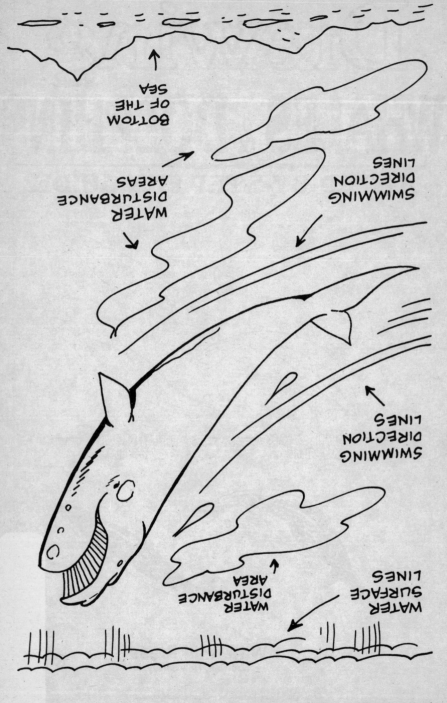

TO MAKE YOUR PICTURES MORE
INTERESTING — ADD —

BOTTOM OF THE SEA

WATER DISTURBANCE AREAS

SWIMMING DIRECTION LINES

SWIMMING DIRECTION LINES

WATER DISTURBANCE AREA

WATER SURFACE LINES

DRAWING TIPS

ALWAYS DRAW THE FIRST **2** STEPS LIGHTLY IN PENCIL UNTIL YOU ARE SATISFIED WITH THE WAY IT LOOKS.

DON'T BE AFRAID TO ERASE!

① JUST DRAW BASIC SHAPE

② START TO ADD BASIC DETAILS

BOTTLE-NOSED DOLPHIN

③ ERASE GUIDE LINES AND FINISH YOUR DRAWING

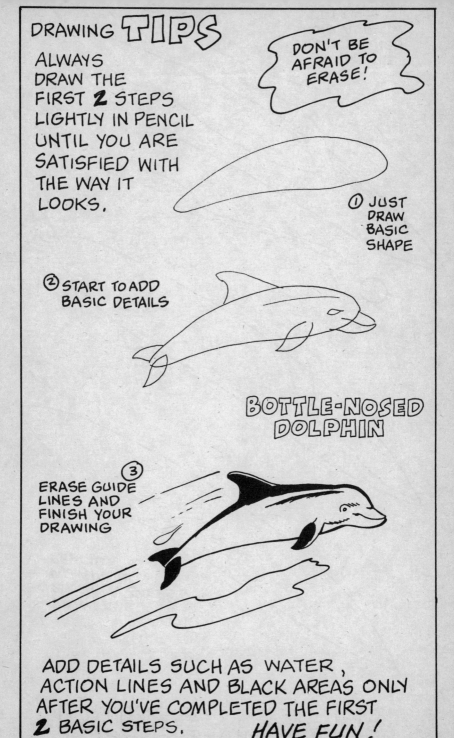

ADD DETAILS SUCH AS WATER, ACTION LINES AND BLACK AREAS ONLY AFTER YOU'VE COMPLETED THE FIRST **2** BASIC STEPS. *HAVE FUN!*

BYRDE'S WHALE

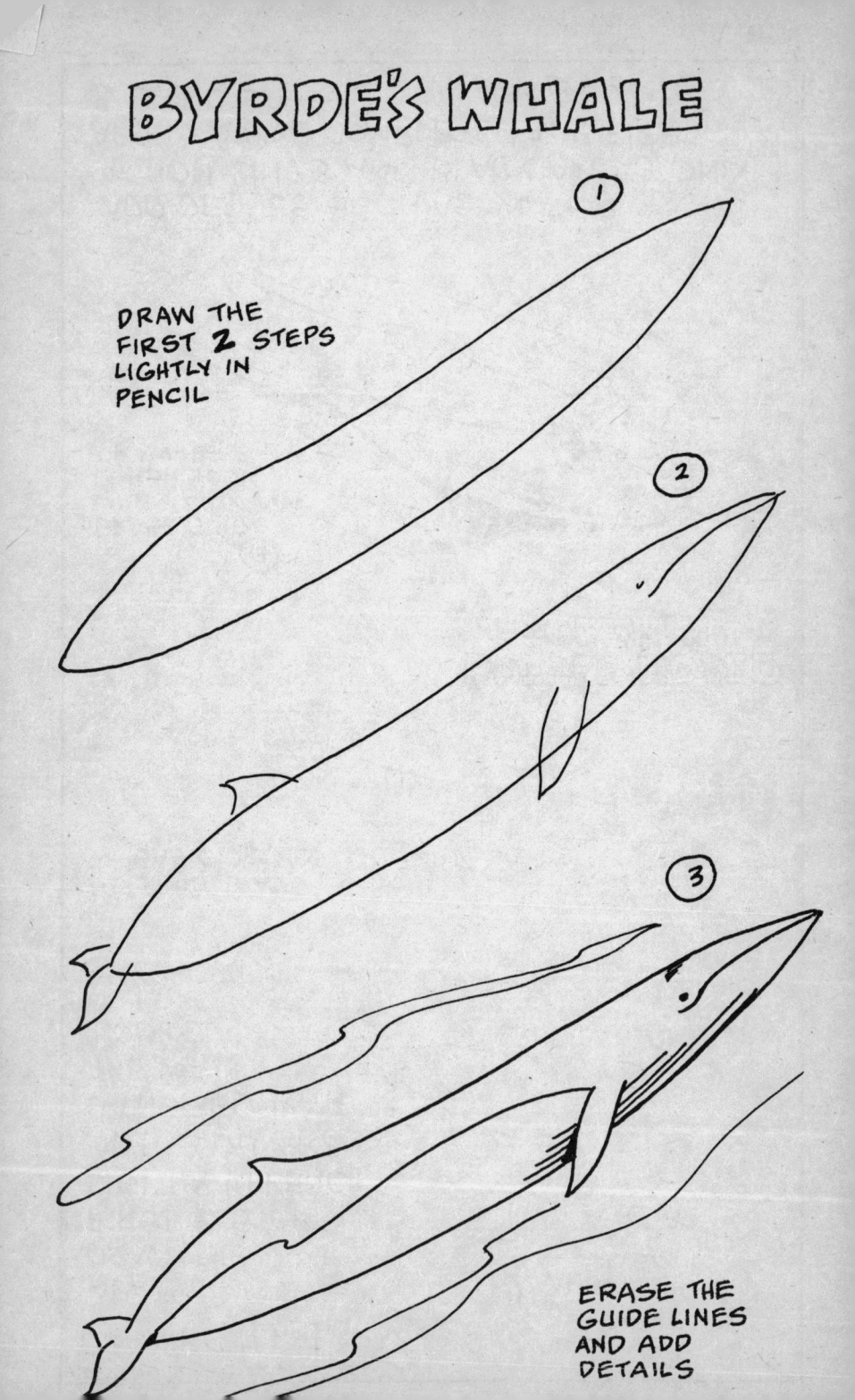

DRAW THE
FIRST **2** STEPS
LIGHTLY IN
PENCIL

ERASE THE
GUIDE LINES
AND ADD
DETAILS

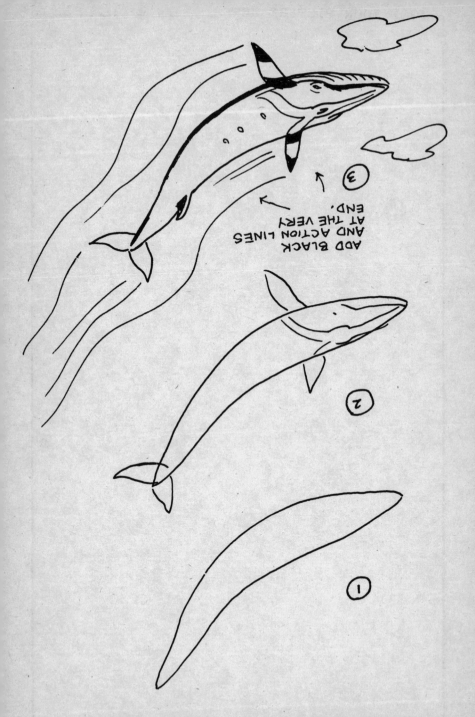

ADD BLACK
AND ACTION LINES
AT THE VERY
END.

① ② ③

MINKE WHALE

BOWHEAD WHALE

1

2

ADD WATER
SURFACE AND ACTION LINES.

3

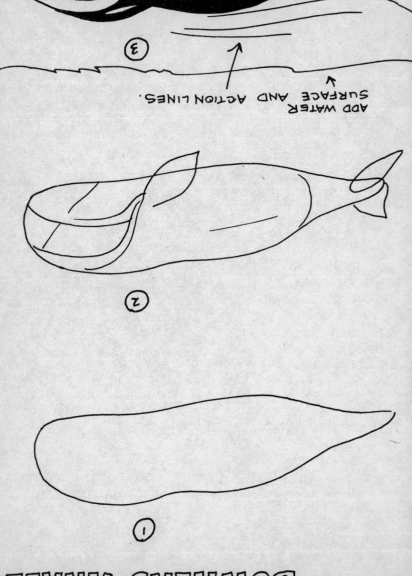

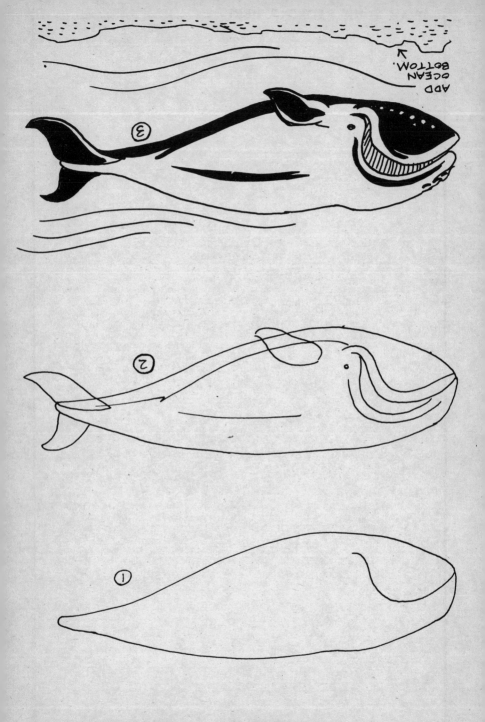

RIGHT WHALE

DRAW YOUR PICTURE HERE

BLUE WHALE

SPERM WHALE

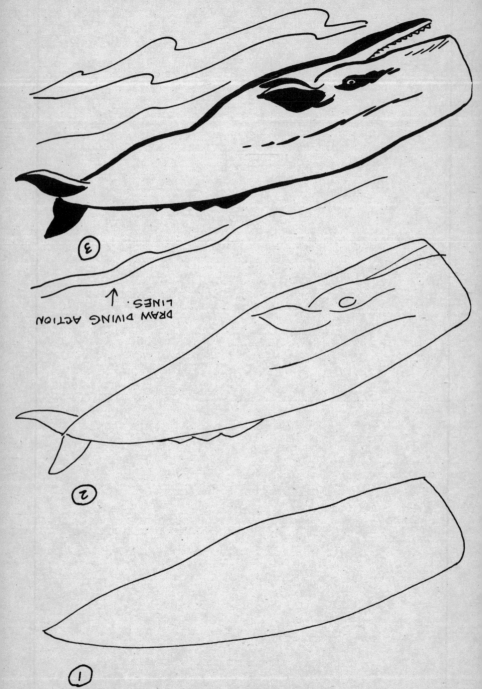

DRAW DIVING ACTION LINES.

1

2

3

FIN WHALE

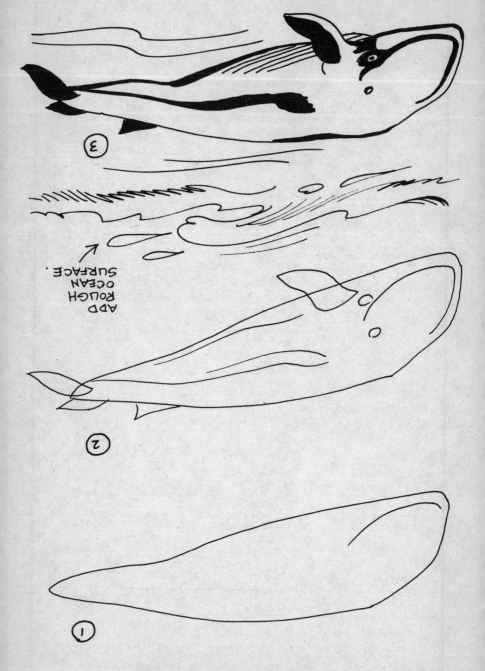

1

2

ADD ROUGH OCEAN SURFACE.

3

DRAW YOUR PICTURE HERE

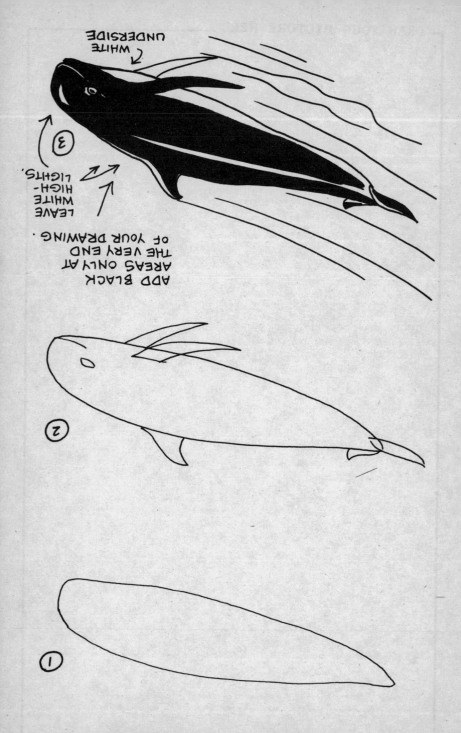

PILOT WHALE

1

2

3

ADD BLACK
AREAS ONLY AT
THE VERY END
OF YOUR DRAWING.

LEAVE
WHITE
HIGH-
LIGHTS.

WHITE UNDERSIDE

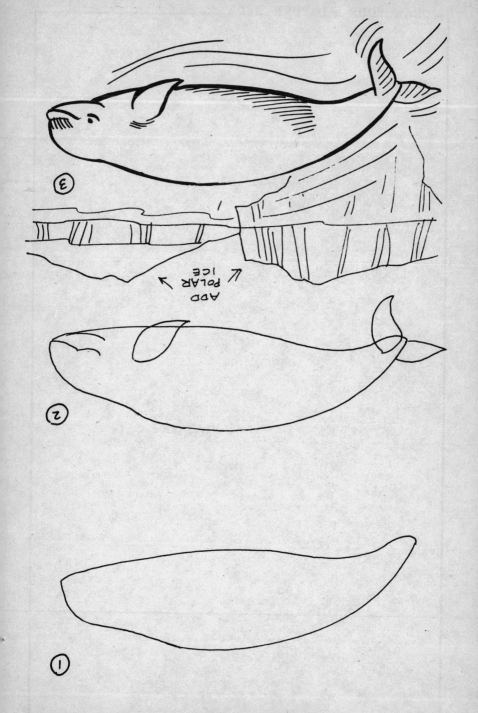

BELUGA WHALE

1

2

ADD
POLAR
ICE

3

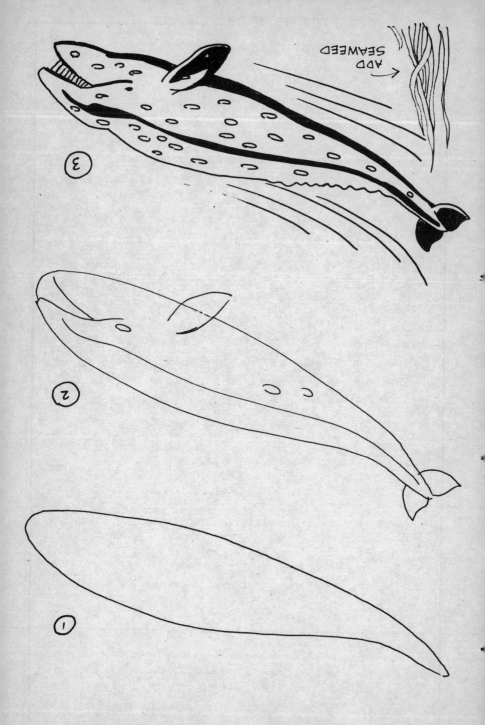

GRAY WHALE

1

2

3

ADD SEAWEED

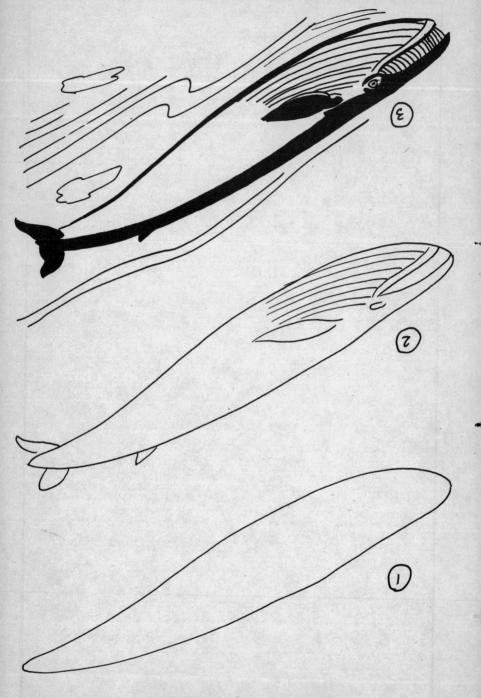

FIN WHALE

1

2

3

KILLER WHALE

1

2

3

DRAW IT BURSTING
OUT OF THE WATER.

HUMPBACK WHALE

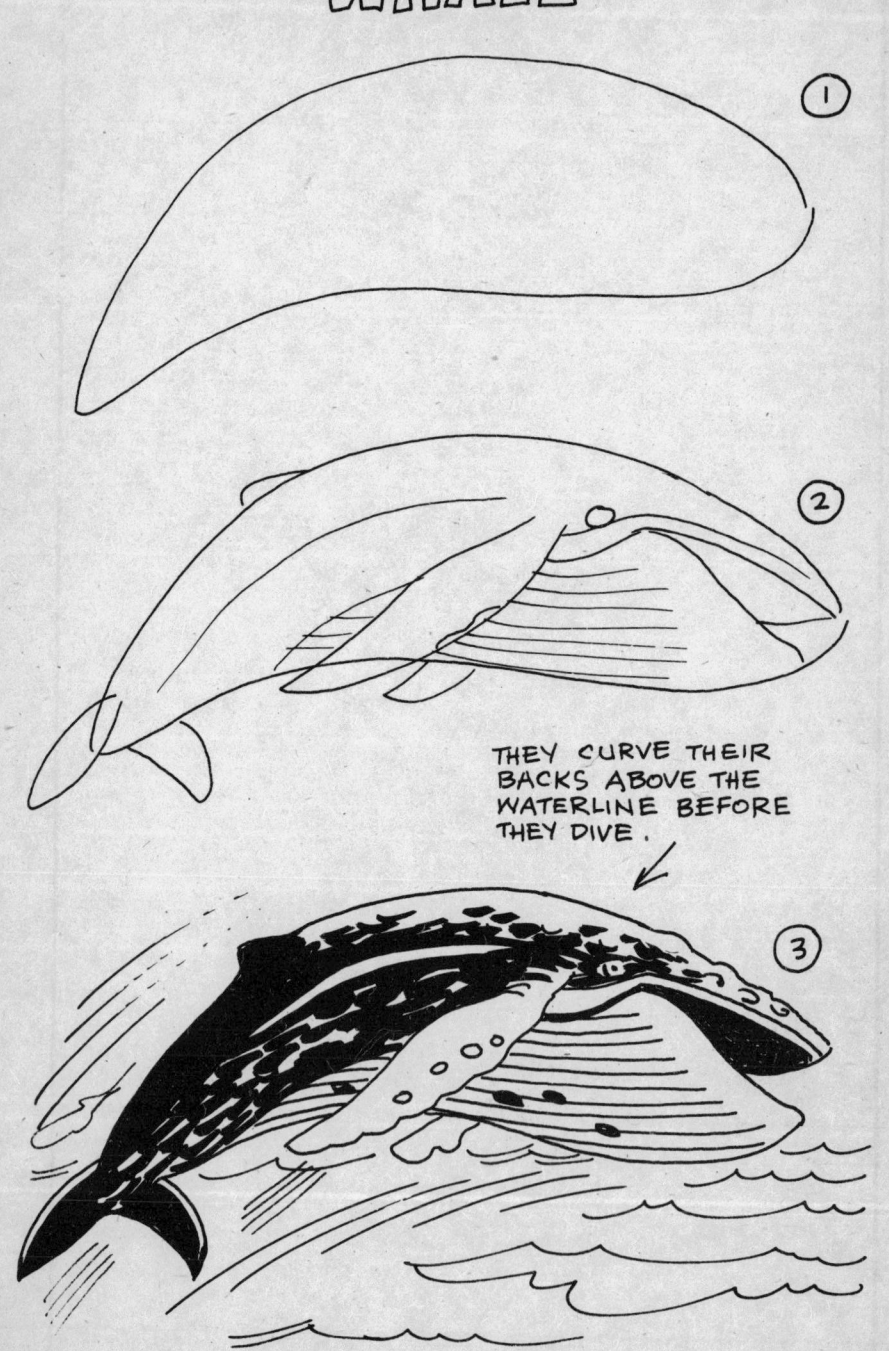

THEY CURVE THEIR
BACKS ABOVE THE
WATERLINE BEFORE
THEY DIVE.

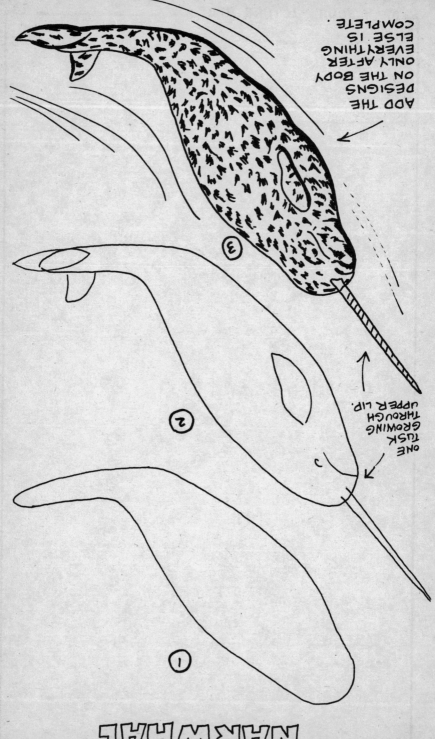

NARWHAL

ADD THE DESIGNS ON THE BODY ONLY AFTER EVERYTHING ELSE IS COMPLETE.

ONE TUSK GROWING THROUGH UPPER LIP.

1

2

3

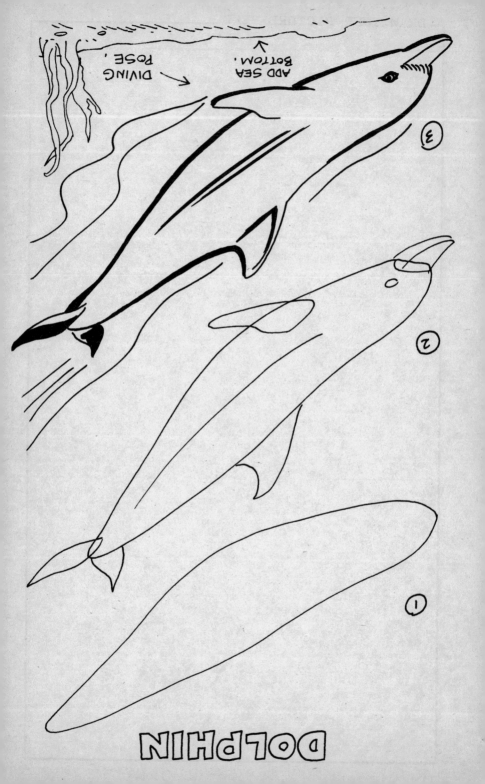

DOLPHIN

1

2

3

ADD SEA
BOTTOM.

DIVING
POSE.

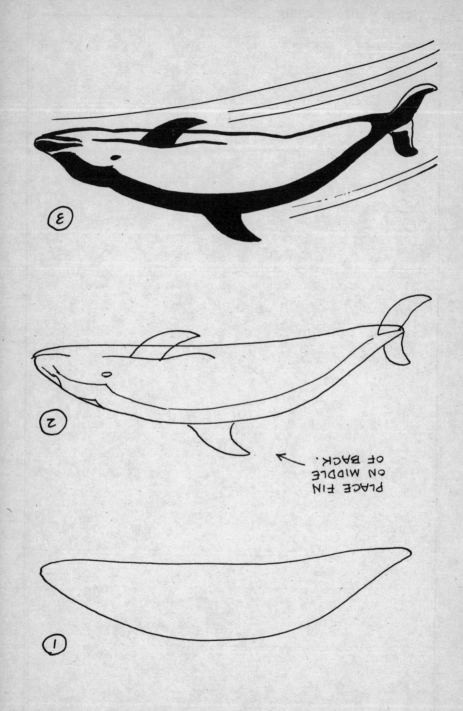

DOLPHIN

①

②

PLACE FIN
ON MIDDLE
OF BACK.

③

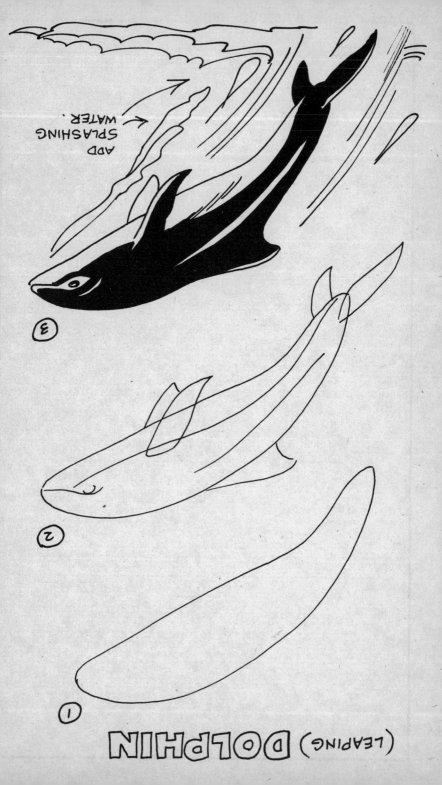

DOLPHIN (LEAPING)

1

2

3

ADD SPLASHING WATER.

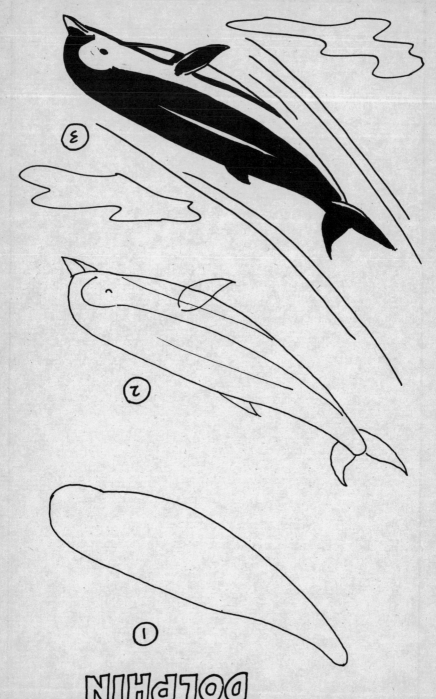

BOTTLE-NOSED
DOLPHIN
(DIVING)

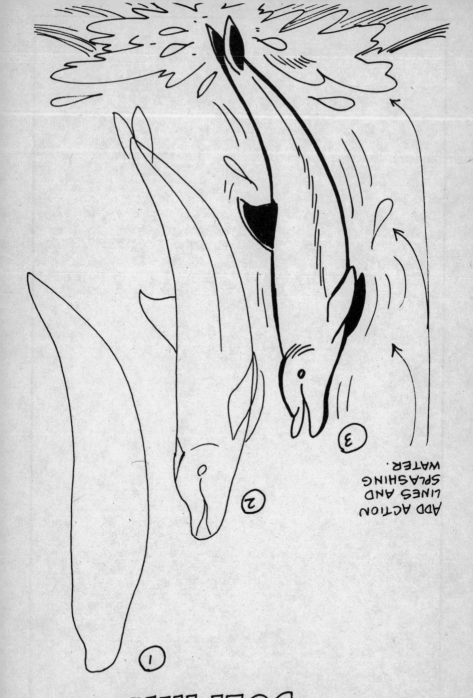

BOTTLE-NOSED DOLPHIN
(IN A WATER SHOW)

① ② ③

ADD ACTION LINES AND SPLASHING WATER.

BOTTLE-NOSED
DOLPHIN
(LEAPING)

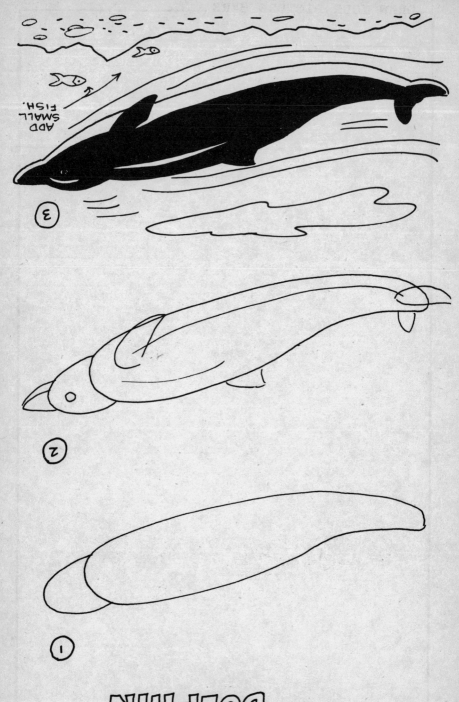

ADD SMALL FISH.

③

②

①

BOTTLE-NOSED DOLPHIN

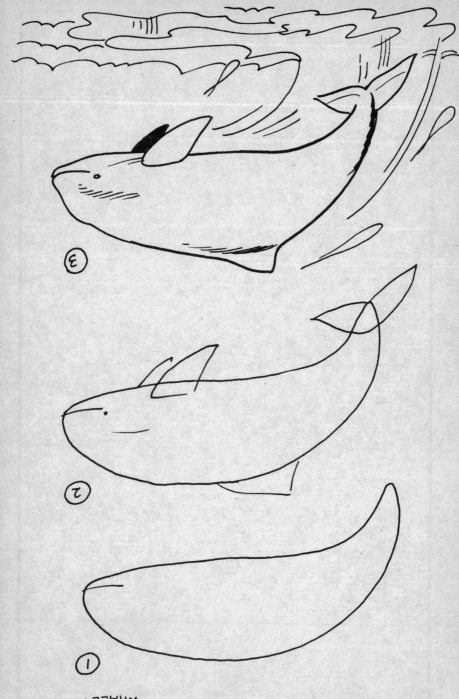

PORPOISE IS REALLY A SMALL TOOTHED WHALE.

DRAW YOUR OWN WHALE OR DOLPHIN PICTURE HERE.